best of British

ABOUT THE AUTHOR

As an integral part of the judges' panel on ITV's *Britain's Best Dish*, Ed Baines knows what Britain eats today. Classically trained, Ed started his career at The Dorchester. He then spent several years working in France, Italy and Australia and, upon returning to London, he worked at top ranking restaurants like the chic Armani Café, Bibendum and The River Café. He was executive chef at Daphne's before starting his own restaurant in Soho, Randall & Aubin, which has been a great success for the past twelve years. Ed made several TV series for both the BBC and ITV. He appeared on *Great Food Live* and *Ready Steady Cook*, was a frequent guest on BBC1's *Saturday Kitchen* and is a regular on *Daily Cook's Challenge*. His first book, *Entertain*, was published in 2001 and he has been profiled by a range of newspapers and magazines.

best of British

ED BAINES

KYLE BOOKS ◆ PHOTOGRAPHY BY LISA LINDER

This paperback edition first published in Great Britain in 2012 by Kyle Books
an imprint of Kyle Cathie Ltd
23 Howland Street
London, W1T 4AY
www.kylebooks.com

First published in hardback in 2008 by Kyle Cathie Ltd

ISBN: 978 0 85783 088 3

A CIP catalogue record for this title is available from the British Library

Project editor: Suzanna de Jong
Photography: Lisa Linder
Design: Lawrence Morton
Copy editor: Anna Hitchin
Proofreader: Caroline Ball
Indexer: Alex Corrin
Home economists: Sue Ashworth, Annabel Hartog and Lucinda Kaizik
Props: Susie Clegg
Production: Sha Huxtable

Acknowledgements

First of all I would like to say thank you to my mum for handing over her collection of recipe notes which she'd gathered from the early Sixties onwards. They were extremely helpful as a foundation and a guide to the traditional British dishes in this book. Thank you to the chefs I met in India who showed me quite a few authentic recipes while I was out there. Thanks to Marcel and Suave – you're inspirational. To my three sons whom I practice my home cooking on and who give me feedback, whether too sweet or too spicy. Thanks, of course, to my business partner and the restaurant manager at Randall & Aubin. Thanks again to Kyle for taking me up on this idea and giving me the opportunity to publish this book. Finally, thank you to all of Great Britain for what we eat today.

Introduction   *Best of British* is a cookbook that celebrates the food we eat in Britain today. As a nation that is traditionally modest, we often undersell the fantastic quality of our local British produce – meat, fish, fruit and vegetables. We're also incredibly fortunate to be able to complement this produce with spices and flavourings from all over the world.

When I was asked to be a judge on ITV's *Britain's Best Dish*, now in its sixth season, I was given the incredible opportunity to gain insight into what people all over Britain are cooking at home. This sparked an enormous enthusiasm in me to create new recipes, and also to be inspired by the wonderful dishes that I came across during filming. The thing that has really struck me, having worked on this project for two years, was the huge diversity of dishes that make up the modern British kitchen. The dishes that were put before me to judge ranged from the truly classic – Sunday roasts, game, pies and steamed puddings – to recipes that represent the multicultural society we live in, such as delicious curries, Chinese-influenced flavours and spicy Caribbean dishes. They all make up the melting pot of culinary Britain today. The diversity of our palates and our broad-minded approach to new flavours make this country a unique foodie nation.

The majority of the recipes in this book will be familiar to you, but I believe many people won't know how to make them at home. There is enormous nostalgia for some of our great dishes, but at the same time, unfortunately, they are not enjoyed as they should be. Our great pies and puddings, for instance, are often eaten as microwaved concoctions, pastry comes from a packet in the freezer and classics from curry to fish and chips come from a takeaway.

You may ask yourself (or me), why should you go to the trouble to make a pie, bake fresh scones or boil a ham when you can get it ready made. My answer is that there is nothing better! Just imagine a homemade pastry with a wonderful meat and fresh vegetable filling served as a supper dish… And when it comes to a homemade curry, all I can say is, it really is a different kettle of fish. Try making the recipes in this book yourself and they may trigger wonderful memories of what your mother or grandmother used to cook.

The best of British cooking isn't just about riches from the past, though; it includes a wide range of different ethnic influences. I genuinely believe the curries, patties, Chinese and Caribbean dishes I've selected for the book are some of the finest you'll be able to make – these are dishes that easily fit the description of British food in the 21st century.

The recipes have been broken down into what felt to me like natural chapters – hot and cold starters, fish, meat and poultry, puddings and the like. There are separate chapters for pies, curries and teatime. I hope this enables you to easily select the recipe that takes your fancy. I've created recipes that are straightforward to follow, relatively quick to prepare and use simple techniques. The only real skill you need to make them is patience. I believe them to be enormously rewarding to make and, of course, delicious to eat.

Enjoy.

ED BAINES

The perfect bacon sandwich

Although for different recipes it's best to use different varieties, I think for this recipe, dry-cured smoked back bacon works best.

SERVES 1

1 good-quality soft tomato, halved and thinly sliced

good salt and freshly ground black pepper

olive oil

a handful of salad leaves, such as baby spinach

1 tablespoon mayonnaise

juice of ¼ lemon

4 rashers of bacon

2 slices of country bread

½ teaspoon wholegrain mustard

Put the tomato into a bowl, add a good pinch of salt and a tablespoon of olive oil.

In a separate bowl, mix the salad leaves with the mayonnaise, lemon juice and a good pinch of black pepper.

Allow both the tomato and the salad leaves to sit while you prepare the bacon and bread – it's vital that you do this first to allow the tomato to stand in the salt and the lettuce to wilt a little with the mayonnaise.

Put 2 rashers of bacon on top of each slice of bread. Whack them under the grill on a medium heat – cooking the bacon slowly means that the bacon juices run out on to the bread. It also makes the bacon very crisp.

When the bread is toasted, remove it from the grill and put to one side. Turn the bacon and cook for a further 3 to 4 minutes.

Place the cooked bacon rashers onto a slice of toasted bread. Cover with a handful of the lettuce and scoop over the tomatoes with all the juices. Smear the mustard over the other piece of bread. Place on top of the sandwich, squeeze down, cut in half and enjoy.

Sausage fritters with quails' eggs

SERVES 2

2 large Maris Piper potatoes, peeled

1 onion, finely chopped

vegetable oil

6 quails' eggs

1 tablespoon flour

salt

pinch of cayenne pepper

1 teaspoon flour, plus extra for
   dusting

200g sausages

2 tablespoons sultanas

1 tablespoon pork or duck fat

4 sage leaves

1 teaspoon English mustard

1 tablespoon marmalade

Boil the potatoes gently, then mash them and set aside to cool completely. Fry the onion in a little vegetable oil.

Set a kitchen timer and soft-boil the eggs (I give them 2 minutes and 16 seconds). Once boiled, lightly crack the shell of the eggs all over. Hold the eggs, one by one, under gently running water while you very carefully peel them.

Add the flour, a good pinch of salt and the cayenne pepper to the cold mashed potato. Work together to form a dough. Dust a chopping board with some flour. Roll and shape the potato mixture into golf ball-sized pieces. Press flat to create small cakes and chill in the fridge for 30 minutes.

Meanwhile, split open the sausage skins and squeeze out the meat. Thoroughly mix the fried onions and sultanas into the meat. Dust the chopping board with some more flour and roll the meat mixture into golf ball-sized balls. Press flat into cakes – these are your fritters.

Put the fat into a large frying pan and fry the potato cakes over a medium heat. Make sure that, when you add the cakes, you gently move them in the pan so that they don't stick. When cooked, remove and place on a plate. Keep warm under a low grill.

Fry the sausage fritters in the same pan for 4 to 5 minutes. Turn over and cook on the other side. Add the sage leaves to the pan at this point. Remove the potato cakes from under the grill, cover with the fritters and cooked sage leaves and place under the grill again to keep warm.

Wipe out the pan with some kitchen paper. Pour in 2 tablespoons of water, the mustard and the marmalade. Bring gently to the boil, stirring until you have a smooth syrup.

Arrange the fritters and potato cakes on individual plates. Spoon over the syrup and finish with the quails' eggs, cut in half.

Ham and eggs with toasted fruit bread

Although it seems a strange combination, the savoury flavours of the ham and egg work wonderfully well with the sweetness of fruit bread.

SERVES 1

2 slices of honey and mustard ham

1 tablespoon pork fat or vegetable oil

2 eggs

2 slices of fruit bread (see page 221)

25g butter, softened

With a sharp knife, make a cut three-quarters of the way through each slice of ham. Overlap the cut edges to form a cone.

Gently heat the fat or oil in a pan. Place the ham cones in the pan and heat through for 1 minute. Tilt the pan away from you and push the two pieces of ham to the far edge of the pan, with the cone opening pointing towards you. Crack an egg into each cone and hold the pan pointing downwards until the eggs start to set.

Place the pan back flat on a heat for 5 minutes until the eggs are cooked through. Occasionally spoon hot oil from the pan over the eggs.

Toast the fruit bread – beware, it cooks very quickly. Butter the bread, and gently top each slice with a ham and egg cone.

Braised tomatoes on muffins

SERVES 2

2 tablespoons pork fat or vegetable oil

1 garlic clove, finely sliced

4 anchovy fillets

zest of 1 lemon

6 ripe tomatoes

½ teaspoon sugar

2 muffins, sliced in half

butter

salt

2 sprigs of fresh thyme, to garnish

In a large saucepan, gently heat the fat or oil over a moderate heat. Add the garlic and anchovy fillets. Stir constantly until the anchovy fillets have dissolved. Remove from the heat and stir in the lemon zest.

Cut the tomatoes in quarters. Place the saucepan back on the heat and add the tomatoes to the mixture with the sugar. Cook gently for 25 minutes, stirring occasionally.

Just before serving, toast and butter the muffins.

Serve the braised tomatoes on top of the hot muffins. Season with salt and garnish with a sprig of thyme.

Curried eggs and rice

This is a great dish – you can also add pieces of
either smoked mackerel or kippers to the rice sauce
and egg mixture if you like.

SERVES 4

1 tablespoon cumin seeds

vegetable oil

pinch of red chilli powder

1 tablespoon onion flakes

pinch of salt

pinch of sugar

2 cups basmati rice, rinsed

juice of 2 limes

4 eggs

FOR THE CURRY SAUCE

50g butter

1 onion, finely chopped

1 garlic clove, crushed

thumb-sized piece of fresh ginger,
  grated

¼ tablespoon turmeric

½ teaspoon garam masala

½ teaspoon cinnamon

½ teaspoon chaat masala

100ml vegetable stock (see page
  230)

400ml yoghurt

salt and freshly ground black pepper

First make the curry sauce. Melt the butter in a saucepan. Add the onion and gently soften, then add the garlic and most of the ginger. Stir in the turmeric, garam masala, cinnamon and chaat masala and cook for 1 minute.

Gradually stir in the vegetable stock. Bring to the boil and reduce by half. Remove from the heat, allow to cool and then add the yoghurt. Place in a blender and whiz until smooth, then season.

Toast the cumin seeds in a dry frying pan, then crush them in a pestle and mortar. Heat 2 tablespoons vegetable oil in a large saucepan and add the cumin, chilli powder, onion flakes, remaining ginger and the sugar and salt. Cook for 1 minute. Add the rice and 4 cups of water, bring to the boil and cover. Cook gently until all the liquid is absorbed by the rice.

Drain the rice in a colander. Put the rice back in the pan and pop on the lid to allow the rice to steam and become light and fluffy.

Soft-boil the eggs for 4 minutes, then place in a bowl of cold water and allow to cool. Once the eggs are nice and cold, very gently remove the shell so that they don't split. Place to one side.

Reheat the sauce and allow it to reduce by a third, stirring occasionally. Warm through the rice with the eggs on top. Serve with the sauce spooned over.

Kipper with chive and lemon butter

SERVES 1

1 large kipper
75g butter
1 large shallot, finely
  chopped
25ml water
½ large lemon
bunch of fresh chives,
  finely sliced
pinch of white pepper

Place the kipper in a large frying pan, skin side down. Gently place 1 teaspoon of butter on the kipper and place under a hot grill. Butter the brown bread.

Cook the fish all the way through – this will take 3 to 4 minutes. For the last couple of minutes, turn down to a medium heat.

Lift the kipper on to a chopping board. Remove and discard the central bone. Place the kipper on a plate, ready to serve.

Place the frying pan with its fish juices on to a gentle heat and fry the shallots until softened. Add the water and turn the heat up to full whack. Bring to the boil and add the remaining butter, the lemon juice and chives. This should combine to make a rich sauce.

Spoon the sauce over the kipper and serve with buttered brown bread.

ED'S TIP It's a sacrilege to buy vacuum-packed kipper fillets from the supermarket – they taste nothing like a proper kipper!

Smoked salmon and poached eggs on muffins

Although this is not the classic, French way of poaching an egg, it works just as well and avoids the use of vinegar, which I find taints the flavour of the eggs in this particular recipe.

SERVES 2

salt and white pepper

4 eggs

2 muffins, sliced in half

butter

250g smoked salmon

Place a frying pan on the hob and fill it two-thirds full with boiling water from the kettle. Add ½ teaspoon of salt. Adjust the heat to medium and crack the eggs into the water. They will resemble the shape and form of fried eggs.

When the water starts to bubble, turn it down to the lowest possible heat. Allow to cook gently.

Meanwhile, grill or toast the muffins until lightly browned on both sides. Spread with butter and top with smoked salmon. Place back under the grill and cook the smoked salmon until it takes on a pale-but-just-browning appearance. (In my opinion, eating raw smoked salmon with hot eggs is something gone wrong along the way...)

Remove the muffins from under the grill. Using a spatula, lift the eggs from the pan and place one egg on top of each muffin. Sprinkle with a little salt and some white pepper. Quickly flash under the grill for 1 minute and serve.

Pilchards in a curry sauce

Pilchards is the Cornish name for sardines. In the old days, they were fished in abundance and stock rapidly declined. In recent years the numbers have been increasing again, and now pilchards/sardines are available at just about every fish counter. Pilchards are a fantastic source of good fatty acids such as omega-3 and, like all breakfast fish dishes, it really sets you up with a positive state of mind to start the day.

SERVES 2

4 tablespoons vegetable oil

1 teaspoon garam masala

¼ teaspoon dried chilli

¼ teaspoon ground mace

good pinch of celery salt

1 small onion, chopped

2 garlic cloves, chopped

175g pilchard fillets

juice of 1 lime

2 slices of sourdough bread

butter

1 teaspoon creamed horseradish, to
  serve

Heat the oil in a frying pan and add all the dried spices. Turn down to a low heat, add the onion and garlic. Cook very gently for 5 minutes.

Add the pilchard and the lime juice to the pan. Cook very gently for 10 minutes. Remove from the heat and allow to cool.

Toast the slices of bread and lightly butter them. Place the fish on top and serve with a little creamed horseradish on the side.

ED'S TIP Any good crusty bread would be good here, but you'll find me recommending sourdough bread a lot, as I really like it – see page 210 for the recipe.

Creamed haddock and leeks on muffins

SERVES 2

50g butter

2 large leeks, thoroughly rinsed and
   finely sliced

4 anchovy fillets, finely sliced

300ml milk

225g smoked haddock fillets

small bunch of curly parsley

zest and juice of ½ lemon

200ml double cream

2 hard-boiled eggs, grated

salt and freshly ground black pepper

75g grated Cheddar cheese

1 teaspoon creamed horseradish

2 muffins, halved

wedges of lemon, to serve

Gently melt the butter in a saucepan. Add the leeks and anchovies to the butter and fry over a moderate heat until completely softened.

Meanwhile, pour the milk into a large frying pan. Bring to simmering point and lay the haddock fillets, skin side up, in the pan. Cook gently for 10 minutes and turn off. Allow the fish to cool in the pan.

Add the parsley to the cooked leeks, then stir the lemon zest and juice. Bring to the boil, then add the cream. Bring back to the boil and remove from the heat.

Lift the fish out of the pan, remove the skin and bones and discard. Flake the fish and add to the leek with the eggs and some seasoning. Finally, stir in the cheese and horseradish. Allow the mixture to cool.

Toast the muffins. Spoon the creamed haddock and leeks over the toasted muffins and place under a hot grill until golden brown. Serve with a wedge of lemon.

Smoked mackerel and scrambled eggs

If you're making this for two, three or four lucky people, scale up ingredients accordingly.

SERVES 1

2 large eggs

25ml single cream

pinch of salt and white pepper

25g butter

75g smoked mackerel fillet, skin
   removed and flesh gently flaked

2 slices of sourdough bread

wedge of lemon, to serve

Crack the eggs into a large bowl. Gently whisk in the cream. It's important that it's thoroughly mixed, but don't incorporate too much air. Season with salt.

Add the butter to a medium-sized non-stick frying pan and allow it to melt over a moderate heat. Add the mackerel and warm through by moving it around in the pan.

Remove the pan from the heat while you toast the bread.

Place the pan back on the heat, and pour in the egg and cream mixture immediately. Stir with a spatula in a gentle but constant movement around the pan (you'll need to work quickly – the eggs will only need 35 to 50 seconds to cook).

Remove the pan from the heat while the eggs are still a little loose. The scrambled eggs should be large and chunky, not small popcorn-like nuggets.

Serve the eggs on the sourdough toast. Season with pepper and serve with a wedge of lemon.

Crispy lemon sole with anchovy sauce

SERVES 2

pinch of celery salt

pinch of ground cumin

pinch of cayenne pepper

100g flour

salt and white pepper

4 lemon sole fillets

1 teaspoon white wine vinegar

100ml single cream

vegetable oil

2 eggs

2 slices of sourdough bread

FOR THE ANCHOVY SAUCE

50g butter

1 teaspoon Gentleman's Relish

1 tablespoon chopped fresh parsley,
  plus 2 sprigs to serve

juice of ½ lemon

For the anchovy butter, put the butter, Gentleman's Relish and chopped parsley into a saucepan and heat, stirring, until the butter has melted. Place to one side.

Add all the spices to the flour with a pinch of salt and pepper. Roll the fish in the seasoned flour and leave it to sit for 1 minute – this will allow the flour to bind to the surface of the fish.

Half-fill a saucepan with water. Add a pinch of salt and the white wine vinegar. Place over a low heat.

While the water heats up, remove the fish from the flour and dip into the cream. Put the fish back in the flour and thoroughly coat.

Heat 2 tablespoons vegetable oil in a frying pan on a moderate heat. Add the fish fillets, one at a time, to the pan, shaking it as you go to ensure that they don't stick to the bottom. Turn with a pallet knife and cook on the other side, then remove to and drain on kitchen paper.

Once the water boils, turn it up to a full heat and, using a whisk, create a whirlpool in the water. Crack the eggs one by one into the centre – the eggs will swirl around. Reduce to a low heat and let the eggs cook for 2 minutes.

Meanwhile, toast the sourdough bread, put on to individual plates and place an egg on top of each piece. Gently place 2 sole fillets on top of each egg.

Bring the anchovy sauce back up to the boil and whisk in the lemon juice. Pour this over the sole fillets and poached eggs. Serve with a sprig of fresh parsley.

ED'S TIP Use any flat fish you like instead of sole, such as plaice or flounder.

Smoked cod roe with lemon butter

SERVES 2

4 slices of sourdough bread

2 large ripe tomatoes, halved

100g smoked cod roe

pinch of cayenne pepper

FOR THE LEMON BUTTER

50g butter

zest and juice of 1 large lemon

To make the lemon butter, melt the butter in a pan and stir in the lemon zest and juice.

Toast the bread on both sides. Leave the grill on. Gently spoon some of the melted lemon butter on to the toasted bread. Vigorously rub the bread with the tomatoes, squeezing at the same time. Bin the remains of the tomatoes.

Split the cod roe and sprinkle with the cayenne pepper. Using a knife, spread it over the slices of bread. Place under the grill and warm through for a couple of minutes. Finish by drizzling over any remaining lemon butter and serve.

Ham and peas with Lincolnshire cheese

It may seem odd to eat peas for breakfast, but if you're starting early and have a big day ahead of you, this one really sets you up. And enjoy it with a warming pot of tea too.

SERVES 2

300g peas

150g Lincolnshire cheese, roughly
  grated

good pinch of pepper

2 egg yolks

1 teaspoon Worcestershire sauce

½ teaspoon English mustard

2 slices of good quality bread

25g butter

2 thick slices of good-quality ham,
  ideally homemade (see page 73)

In a bowl, combine the peas, cheese, pepper, egg yolks, Worcestershire sauce and mustard. Place to one side.

Lightly grill or toast the bread on both sides and brush with the butter. Place to one side.

Heat a non-stick frying pan on a moderate heat. Dry-fry the ham gently for about 1 minute on each side. Place the ham on the toasted bread and spoon over the pea and cheese mixture.

Place it under a hot grill until the cheese is gooey, bubbling and golden brown.

Coddled eggs

You won't have time to do this if you're in a rush in the morning, but it's a great one for weekends.

SERVES 2
50g butter
8 button mushrooms, finely sliced
75g smoked ham, chopped
1 teaspoon English mustard
4 tablespoons single cream
salt and white pepper
2 very fresh hens' or ducks' eggs
2 slices of sourdough bread, to serve

Preheat the oven to 180°C/350°F/gas mark 4.

Gently melt the butter in a saucepan, making sure you avoid burning it. Add the mushrooms and gently cook, stirring constantly, for 3 to 4 minutes.

Mix in the ham and warm through for 1 minute. Stir in the mustard and 2 tablespoons of the cream, then add a pinch of salt and pepper.

Spoon the ham and mushroom mixture into two small ramekins, dividing it equally. Pour off the excess butter – set it aside to serve over the sourdough toast later. Spoon a tablespoon of cream into each ramekin.

Crack an egg over each ramekin. Place in the oven and cook for 12 to 15 minutes.

While these are cooking, toast the sourdough bread. Pour the reserved flavoured butter over the toasted slices and serve them with the eggs.

Swansea jacks

These are traditional Welsh breakfast cakes from Swansea.

SERVES 4
675g baking potatoes, peeled and
  diced coarsely
1 large onion, finely chopped
vegetable oil
225g laver bread (see tip below)
potato flour, for dusting
225g porridge oats, seasoned
salt and freshly ground black pepper
4 poached eggs, to serve (see page
  20)

Boil the potatoes in salted water for 20 minutes. Meanwhile, brown the onion in oil.

Drain the cooked potatoes, mash them and add the onions and cooked laver bread. Allow to cool. Dust a work surface with potato flour, sprinkle over the oats and season them with salt and pepper.

Shape the potato mixture into golf ball-sized cakes and roll them in the porridge oats. Shallow fry until golden brown and serve with the eggs.

ED'S TIP: Laver bread is a traditional Welsh delicacy made from this seaweed called laver and is also known as seaweed bread. If you can't buy it pre-cooked, soak 2 packets of seaweed in water for 10 minutes, then squeeze dry.

Pancakes with syrup

MAKES ABOUT 12 PANCAKES

250g plain flour

good pinch of salt

2 eggs

1 teaspoon vegetable oil, plus extra
   for frying

300ml whole milk

50g unsalted butter, melted

handful of blueberries, raspberries,
   blackcurrants or dried fruits

softened butter, to serve

FOR THE SYRUP

120g peeled lemon, stoned cherries
   or blackberries

80g white sugar

a squeeze of lemon juice

Put the flour and salt into a large bowl. Make a well in the centre and add the eggs and oil. With a whisk, work the flour into the eggs and oil until a thick paste is formed. Slowly add the milk, beating constantly to prevent any lumps from forming.

Continue until you have a smooth batter, then mix in the melted butter. Leave the batter to rest for at least 15 minutes – an hour would be ideal as it would help the batter hold together better when cooking, and make the pancake crispier.

To make the syrup, put your chosen fruit in a saucepan with the sugar and the squeeze of lemon juice. Bring to the boil and turn down to a low heat. Cook for 40 minutes. Remove from the heat and allow to cool. Blend in a food processor and pass through a fine sieve back into the pan. Bring it back to the boil and pour into a serving jug or sterilised jar (see tip page 235). Stored in the fridge, the syrup will keep for up to 3 weeks.

Here's how to cook the perfect pancake. Preheat the oven to 120°C/250°F/gas mark ½, placing a plate inside to warm up. Stir 50ml of water into the batter just before cooking. Pour some vegetable oil into a non-stick pan and ladle in 30ml of the batter. Allow the batter to spread to the edge of the pan. If you're using a large pan, you can probably cook three pancakes at a time.

At this point, drop your chosen fruits on to the soft top of the pancake. Leave for 45–60 seconds.

Flip the pancake using a pallet knife. Place the cooked pancakes on the plate in the oven until you've created a huge pile. Serve with soft butter and your delicious homemade syrup.

Breakfast drinks

Orange juice fizz

MAKES 1 LITRE
juice of 1 lemon
100ml water
2 tablespoons sugar
juice of 6 oranges (blood oranges are
   great if you can get them)
750ml sparkling water

Put the lemon juice, water and sugar into a pan. Bring to a gentle boil and remove from the heat. Allow to cool.

Stir in the orange juice, then pour through a sieve into a jug. Add the sparkling water and serve.

Get up and go smoothie

Although some of these ingredients aren't strictly British, they are all readily available now so I've adopted them. If you're in a real rush to get out early and want something really healthy to get you through to lunch, this liquid breakfast really does the trick.

SERVES 1
1 banana, sliced
4 tablespoons blueberries (or any
   other berries you've got)
3 tablespoons plain yoghurt
1 heaped tablespoon ground wheat
   or rolled oats (Ready Brek works
   really well)
500ml apple juice
1 tablespoon honey

Add all the ingredients to a blender or food processor. Whiz for 30 seconds, then pour into a pint glass, drink and go.

Sweet lime soda

MAKES 1 LITRE
juice of 1 lemon
100ml water
2 tablespoons sugar
juice of 6 limes
4 ice cubes
750ml soda water

Put the lemon juice, water and sugar into a pan. Bring to a gentle boil and remove from the heat. Allow to cool.

Stir in the lime juice, then pour through a sieve into a blender. Add the ice cubes and whiz for 30 seconds. Pour into a jug, add the soda water and serve.

ED'S TIP: To make grapefruit soda, simply replace the lime juice with the juice of 4 grapefruits.

Nettle squash

This is an oldie but goodie – it seems to have been forgotten about.

MAKES 5 LITRES
2 large lemons, sliced
250g golden syrup
1 teaspoon cream of tartar
2 teaspoons ground ginger
2 handfuls of stinging nettles (or
    about 200 leaves – wear gloves!)
10g yeast

Place the lemon slices in a large bowl. Add the syrup, cream of tartar and ginger.

Clean the nettles, boil them and strain the boiling liquid into the bowl with the lemons in.

Add enough water to make a total of 5 litres. Leave to cool a little, then add the yeast. Leave the liquid until the next day.

Strain and bottle – three large lemonade bottles should do. Leave for at least two days. Like ginger beer, it will go fizzy. If left for three months or more, it will become alcoholic.

Apricot iced tea

You can make iced tea with any fruit tea you fancy. Marry together your chosen flavoured teabag with 2 tablespoons of the same fruit, dried and chopped. This adds a sweetness and depth of flavour that you can't achieve using the tea alone. Always use sugar syrup rather than just sugar; it takes the edge off the bitterness of the tea.

MAKES 1 LITRE
100g dried apricots, chopped
5 apricot-flavoured teabags
750ml spring water

FOR THE SUGAR SYRUP
3 tablespoons sugar
juice of ½ lemon

Bring 250ml tap water to the boil. Drop in the dried fruit and the teabags, boil for 3 minutes and remove from the heat. Put the pan to one side and allow the dried fruit to infuse for 30 minutes.

To make the sugar syrup, bring the sugar and lemon juice to the boil with 150ml tap water. Once the sugar has dissolved, allow it to cool.

Mix together the tea and syrup. Strain through a sieve, add the spring water and chill in the fridge.

Yoghurt with berries and warm honeyed oats

This is a very simple but highly nutritious way to start the day. It should just about carry you through to lunchtime. I always find that when I start the day with a breakfast like this, I'm in a really good mood by 10.30 in the morning. It's particularly good with grapefruit.

SERVES 2

4 tablespoons porridge oats

2 tablespoons honey

200g mixed frozen berries

pinch of salt

1 teaspoon Demerara or unrefined
  sugar

500g fresh yoghurt (ideally Greek)

fresh grapefruit, to serve

Preheat the oven to 150°C/300°F/gas mark 2. Line a large baking tray with greaseproof paper.

Place the oats and honey into a bowl and mix together. Spread the oats over the greaseproof paper, place in the oven and bake for 5 minutes.

Divide the berries into two bowls. Remove the oats from the oven, gently scrape them from the greaseproof paper and sprinkle them over the berries. Add the salt, sugar and stir half the yoghurt into each bowl.

Fresh and dried fruits with honeyed oats

This needs a little forward planning as some preparation should be done the night before. Mind you, if you like it as much as I do, you'll always have some dried fruit soaking with fresh fruit in the fridge, ready to use any time.

SERVES 2

100g dried apricots

50g dried cherries

25g sultanas

100g dried pineapple

100g dried apples

400ml apple juice

1 teaspoon brown sugar

juice of ½ lemon

200g oats

2 tablespoons runny honey

100g fresh grapes, chopped

1 apple, cubed

1 pear, cubed

250g strawberries, chopped into
  quarters

natural yoghurt, to serve

Place all the dried fruits in a large bowl. Pour over the apple juice and stir in the sugar and the lemon juice. Cover with clingfilm and allow to steep in the fridge overnight.

Preheat the oven to 140°C/285°F/gas mark 1½.

Line a baking tray with greaseproof paper. Mix the oats and honey together in a bowl until evenly coated. Scoop the honeyed oats on to the greaseproof paper, spread out evenly and toast in the oven for 15 minutes. Remove and allow to cool.

To serve, combine the fresh fruits with the dried fruits, then add the honeyed oats and toss through quickly. Serve in two bowls and finish with a spoonful of natural yoghurt.

Somerset pasties

Serve with crab apple jelly (see page 234).

SERVES 4

1 small onion, finely chopped

50g celery

50g margarine

1 medium cooking apple, peeled,
  cored and finely chopped

1 teaspoon sugar

225g minced pork

1 tablespoon chopped fresh parsley

pinch of salt

pinch of cayenne pepper

100g Cheddar cheese, grated

4 tablespoons breadcrumbs

1 egg, beaten, for glazing

FOR THE PASTRY

450g plain flour, plus extra for
  dusting

100g cold lard, diced

100g cold butter, diced

pinch of salt

1 tablespoon iced water

To make the pastry, sift the flour into a large bowl. Add the lard, butter and salt. Gently rub together to form a breadcrumb consistency. Add enough iced water to form a dough, ensuring you only use your fingers, and not your hands. Wrap in clingfilm and place in the fridge to rest for 30 minutes.

In a frying pan, fry the onions and celery in the margarine until they start to soften. Add the apple and allow to cook over a moderate heat for 5 minutes. Remove the frying pan from the heat and add the sugar. Transfer the contents of the pan to a bowl and allow to cool.

Preheat the oven to 180°C/350°F/gas mark 4.

Quickly fry the mince until lightly brown and mix with the onion, celery and apple mixture. Stir in the parsley, salt and cayenne.

On a lightly floured surface, roll out the pastry and cut into 12cm rounds. Place a heaped tablespoon of mince mixture into the middle of each pastry round.

Pull up the sides, pressing together and leave a hole at the top.

Fill the hole with the grated cheese and breadcrumbs.

Brush the pastry with the egg. Place the pasties on a baking tray and bake for 30 minutes. Remove from the oven and serve.

Cheese and beer Welsh rarebit

This is delicious, if a little heavy on the cheese. Try it with tomato chutney.

SERVES 4

4 large leeks, thoroughly rinsed and
  very finely chopped

50g butter

1 tablespoon flour

300ml milk

225g mature Cheddar cheese

225g smoked Cheddar cheese

225g Stilton cheese

225g Gloucester cheese

1 egg yolk

2 tablespoons dark ale

few drops of Worcestershire sauce

2 teaspoons mustard

8 slices of soda bread (see page 217)

Cook the leeks in the butter until soft. Add the flour and cook for 1 minute, stirring constantly. Slowly add the milk. Remove from the heat, add all the cheese, the egg yolk, beer, Worcestershire sauce and mustard. Season and mix thoroughly. You must allow this mixture to cool until firm.

Toast the bread slices on one side. Turn over, spoon the chilled rarebit on to the untoasted side. Now grill this side until it is a dark golden brown.

Dorstone goat's cheese with vegetable salad

The best goat's cheese is produced from spring to autumn because this is when goats produce milk. Unlike cows, goats haven't been fooled into breeding throughout the year! I particularly like Dorstone goat's cheese, but if you can't find this, or it is out of season, I suggest you use a good-quality individual goat's cheese. The firmness of the cheese is important – once the centre starts to go soft, it makes it almost impossible to breadcrumb. Just prod it with your fingers before you buy it; it should feel like a ripe avocado.

SERVES 2

2 eggs

100ml milk

200g flour

small bunch of fresh parsley, finely
  chopped

salt and white pepper

1 packet breadcrumbs

1 Dorstone goat's cheese

pinch of sugar

about 500ml vegetable oil, for frying

crab apple jelly (see page 234), to
  serve

FOR THE SALAD

50g dried sour cherries, optional

100ml port

5 small cauliflower florets

1 medium carrot

2 celery sticks

1 teaspoon raspberry vinegar

¼ teaspoon wholegrain mustard

40ml vegetable oil

1 bag mixed small salad leaves

First, if using the dried cherries, put them in the port to infuse it with their delicious flavour. Put the port and cherries in a saucepan on the hob and bring to a gentle boil. Slowly cook down until

reduced by two thirds. Remove from the heat and allow to cool.

You'll need three shallow containers to coat the cheese. Crack the eggs into one container and beat, adding the milk. Mix the flour, parsley and a good pinch of salt and white pepper in another container. Add the breadcrumbs to the third container.

Take a small oven tray and cover with greaseproof paper. Make sure that the cheese is firm and cold. Fill a tall glass with boiling water. Insert a sharp knife into the water and then slice the cheese into 1cm thick rounds.

Gently dust each cheese round in flour, then dip it into the eggs and finally coat with breadcrumbs. Once all the cheese is coated, place the rounds on the greaseproof paper and keep cool. Now clear away any mess as you don't want to get flour, breadcrumbs or raw egg into your salad.

Using a mandolin, finely slice all the vegetables and mix together in a bowl. In another bowl, beat the vinegar, mustard and oil together to form a dressing, then add the cooled cherries and port (this should now be a syrupy texture).

Pour th vegetable oil into a deep-sided saucepan – make sure it doesn't come any higher than halfway up the side of the pan as the level will rise once you lower in the cheese. Heat the oil to 160°C/325°F using a cooking thermometer. Alternatively, drop a clove of garlic into the oil, and when it starts to fizz, the oil is at the right temperature. Remove the garlic clove.

Have ready a slotted spoon and a tray covered in greaseproof paper. Cook the rounds of cheese in two batches and place onto the tray. Once it has all been cooked, remember to turn off the heat under the oil, and push the pot to the back of the hob, handle pointing away from you. Safety first!

Toss the raw vegetables and salad leaves in the dressing. Put a handful of the dressed salad on each plate and top with the cheese.

Serve with crab apple jelly.

Derbyshire cheese and beer fritters

The basis of this recipe is traditionally French and known as *beignets* or *bugnes*. I've anglicised the recipe by substituting ale for water and adding English mustard, Worcestershire sauce and blue cheese.

SERVES 4

150ml local ale

60g butter

70g plain flour, sifted

100g strong local blue cheese, such as Shropshire

1 teaspoon English mustard

1 teaspoon Worcestershire sauce

2 eggs

400ml vegetable oil, for frying

pinch of pepper

bag of mixed salad leaves

large spoonful of local chutney

FOR THE SALAD DRESSING

2 tablespoons cider or herb vinegar

1 teaspoon wholegrain mustard

1 teaspoon honey

6 tablespoons olive oil

pinch of salt and freshly ground black pepper

½ bunch of fresh chives (optional), chopped

Gently heat the beer and butter together until the butter has melted. Add the flour and stir until the mixture leaves the side of the pan. Remove from the heat, add the cheese, mustard and Worcestershire sauce, stirring thoroughly. Allow to cool, then vigorously beat in the eggs, ensuring they are completely amalgamated. Put to one side.

Heat the oil in a deep-sided, sturdy pan. Heat the oil to 160°C/325°F using a cooking thermometer. Alternatively, drop a clove of garlic into the oil, and when it starts to fizz, the oil is at the right temperature. Remove the garlic clove.

Using a tablespoon, gently place spoonfuls of the beer mixture into the hot oil and fry until crisp. Remove and drain on kitchen paper on a plate.

Combine all the dressing ingredients. Pour over the salad leaves, toss and put on a plate. Top with the fritters and finish with a spoonful of chutney.

Red lentil soup with lentil doughnuts

SERVES 4

vegetable oil for frying the spices

2 fresh or freeze-dried curry leaves

2 dried red chillies

1 teaspoon cumin seeds

1 teaspoon mustard seeds

1 red onion, chopped

2 garlic cloves, chopped

2 green chillies, chopped

5 fresh tomatoes, chopped

1 teaspoon grated fresh ginger

1 teaspoon chilli powder

1 teaspoon turmeric

1 teaspoon garam masala

250g red lentils

small bunch of fresh coriander, leaves
   picked

FOR THE DOUGHNUTS

200g black gram lentils

1 tablespoon rice

pinch of salt

pinch of bicarbonate of soda

pinch of baking powder

500ml vegetable oil

For the doughnuts, soak the lentils and rice in warm water for 30 minutes.

To make the soup, heat 2 tablespoons of vegetable oil in a frying pan and gently fry the curry leaves, dried chillies, cumin seeds and mustard seeds for a couple of minutes.

Stir in the onion, garlic and fresh chillies. Add the tomatoes and ginger, followed by the chilli powder, turmeric and garam masala. Add the red lentils and 2 litres of water. Bring to the boil and simmer for 20 to 25 minutes.

Meanwhile, drain the black gram lentils and rice and whiz in a food processor until smooth. Add the salt, bicarbonate of soda and baking powder. Use your hands to shape the mixture into six small patties, poking the middle to create a hole.

Pour the vegetable oil into a deep-sided saucepan – make sure it doesn't come any higher than halfway up the side of the pan as the level will rise once you lower in the fish. Heat the oil to 160°C/325°F using a cooking thermometer. Alternatively, drop a clove of garlic into the oil, and when it starts to fizz, the oil is at the right temperature. Remove the garlic clove.

Gently fry the doughnuts in the hot oil for 5 minutes until lightly browned. Remove and place on to kitchen paper.

Spoon the soup into bowls and serve sprinkled with the fresh coriander leaves and lentil doughnuts on the side.

Potato and leek cakes
with crispy bacon

SERVES 4

550g floury potatoes such as King
  Edwards

100g leeks, thoroughly rinsed and cut
  into 5mm dice

salt and freshly ground black pepper

1 tablespoon bicarbonate of soda

100g plain flour

280ml buttermilk

75g unsalted butter

8 rashers of streaky bacon, each cut
  into 4 pieces

3 sage leaves, shredded

2 teaspoons lemon juice

Boil the potatoes in salted water until tender but not soft. Drain well and leave to cool. Mash half the potatoes and grate the rest coarsely.

Blanch the leeks in salted, boiling water until cooked. Drain in a colander and dry on a tea towel. Sift the bicarbonate of soda and flour and mix in the mashed potato, grated potato and the leeks. Stir in the buttermilk to form a thick batter.

Heat 50g butter in a non-stick frying pan. Spoon in the batter, a tablespoon at a time to make little cakes. Cook for about 2 minutes. Flip over and cook until golden and puffy.

In a separate pan, fry the bacon until crispy, add the remaining butter along with the sage and lemon juice. Mix together and then spoon over the pancakes to serve.

Poached fried chicken with asparagus salad

SERVES 2

1 garlic clove, unpeeled

sprig of fresh rosemary

2 chicken breasts

bunch of asparagus, trimmed of the
  woody bits

5 anchovy fillets

1 teaspoon mustard

2 tablespoons flavoured vinegar
  (whatever's in your cupboard)

olive oil

1 red onion, finely sliced

bunch of spring onions, finely
  chopped

6 tomatoes, finely chopped

250g olives, chopped

handful of salad leaves, to serve

Bring 600ml water to the boil in a large saucepan. Add the garlic and rosemary. Once the water is boiling, add the chicken breasts, cover and remove from the heat. Allow the chicken to cool in the pan.

Blanch the asparagus in the boiling water. Remove when cooked and place in iced water.

Remove the garlic from the poaching water. Squeeze it out of its skin and then mash it with the anchovies. Combine with the mustard, flavoured vinegar, 6 tablespoons olive oil and the red onion. Add the spring onion, tomato and olives. Mix well and chill.

Pat the poached chicken breasts dry. Pan-fry skin side down in a little olive oil until crisp. Turn the breast over and remove the pan from the heat. Allow the chicken to sit in the cooling pan while you prepare your salad.

Put some fresh salad leaves tossed with asparagus on to a plate. Slice the chicken breast and lay over the top. Drizzle over the dressing to serve.

Oxtail soup

SERVES 2

2 oxtails

2 tablespoons flour

50g beef dripping

1 onion, chopped

2 garlic cloves, chopped

2 fresh red chillies, sliced

1 teaspoon sugar

1 teaspoon finely chopped fresh
  rosemary

2 tablespoons finely chopped fresh
  parsley

4 tomatoes, cut into wedges

2 Maris Piper potatoes, cut into 2cm
  cubes

250g runner beans, chopped

salt and freshly ground black pepper

1 bay leaf

Cut the oxtails through the bone into discs and toss them in the flour. Heat half the beef dripping in a large casserole dish over a moderate heat. Brown the oxtail in this, then take out the oxtail.

Add the remaining beef dripping to the casserole and heat over a moderate heat. Add the onion and garlic. Fry for a couple of minutes and then add the chillies, sugar, rosemary and parsley. Lightly fry for 1 minute, before adding the tomatoes, potatoes and beans. Cook for a couple of minutes while stirring.

Add the oxtails back to the dish, add 1.8 litres water, salt and pepper and the bay leaf. Bring gently to the boil and simmer for 1½ to 2 hours.

Quail with a pear and bean salad

SERVES 2

300ml dry cider

1 bay leaf

4 quails

500g green beans, topped and tailed

juice of 1 lemon

½ teaspoon English mustard

pinch of salt

bunch of fresh parsley, finely
chopped

1 garlic clove, finely chopped

1 small onion, finely chopped

olive oil

2 tablespoons flaked almonds,
toasted

2 pears, peeled, cored and cut into 8
wedges

200g baby spinach leaves

Pour the cider and 600ml water into a saucepan. Bring to the boil and add the bay leaf. Place the quails into the liquid, remove from the heat immediately and allow the quails to cool in the liquid for 20 minutes.

While they're cooling, prepare the pear and bean salad. Blanch the green beans in boiling salted water for 4 minutes. Prepare a dressing by mixing together the lemon juice, mustard, salt, parsley, garlic, onion, 100ml olive oil and the almonds.

Drain the beans straight into a large bowl. While still hot, drizzle with enough of the dressing to coat and toss together. Add the wedges of pear and toss again. Place to one side.

Remove the quail from the cooking liquor. With a medium-sized knife, cut out the backbone of the quails and press them flat on to a chopping board. Heat a little oil in a frying pan. Dry the quail and then add to the pan. Pan-fry until brown and crisp on both sides.

Add the spinach leaves to the salad, drizzle with a bit more dressing and toss. Put the salad onto a large serving plate. Pop the quails on top and drizzle over any remaining quail juices.

Tea-smoked duck
with a pear and cheese salad

Although the use of pomegranate might seem alien
to a British recipe, I would argue that I've never
seen a tea-bush grow in England, so although there's
an element of fusion cooking which I detest, this
recipe seems to work really well. This is the type of
dish that Ladies What Lunch eat.

SERVES 4
350g demerara sugar
10g star anise
50g Darjeeling tea
10g finely grated lemon zest
2 Barbary duck breasts

FOR THE SALAD
1 tablespoon walnut oil
1 tablespoon pomegranate syrup
juice of ½ lemon
1 small garlic clove
1 pomegranate, seeds removed
1 ripe Comice pear
bunch of watercress
50g Cheshire cheese

Carefully line the base of a deep, lidded saucepan
with tinfoil, making sure there are no gaps or holes
or you'll ruin your pan. Place a raised grill or rack
inside the pan, so that the raised level is about 10 to
15cm above the foil.

In a food processor, whiz the sugar, star anise, tea
and lemon zest to a fine powder. Sprinkle the
powder all over the base of the prepared dish. Place
the duck breast, fat side down, on to the wire rack.
Cover the pan with the lid.

Place on a moderate heat for 6 to 8 minutes.
Remove the pan from the heat and allow to stand,
with the lid on, for a further 5 minutes. Remove the
duck breasts and place to one side to rest. Your
duck breasts should be smoked and also cooked
now. If you have a particularly large duck breast,
you may need to pan-fry it for a further 2 or 3
minutes until pink.

Meanwhile, place the walnut oil, syrup, lemon
juice and garlic in a bowl and add the pomegranate
seeds and any juice. Mix together into a dressing.
Peel, quarter and thickly slice the pear and toss in
the dressing. Slice the duck breasts.

Place a little watercress on each plate, scatter
over the dressed pear slices, sliced duck and top
with shavings of Cheshire cheese.

Creamy cauliflower soup with cheese scones

SERVES 4

50g butter

1 onion, finely diced

1 leek, thoroughly rinsed and chopped

3 celery sticks, chopped

600ml medium cider

600ml vegetable stock (see page 231)

1 cauliflower, cut into florets

225g blue Stilton cheese, crumbled

salt and freshly ground black pepper

300ml single cream

pinch of mace

pinch of nutmeg

FOR THE SCONES

5 new potatoes, peeled and diced

500g self raising flour plus extra for rolling

½ teaspoon baking powder

salt and freshly ground black pepper

50g butter

50g red Leicester cheese, grated

50g double Gloucester cheese, grated

50g mature Cheddar, grated

10 fresh basil leaves, finely torn (optional)

good pinch of dried sage

1 egg

300ml milk, plus a little extra for glazing

2 tablespoons wholegrain mustard

Gently melt the butter in a saucepan. Cook the onion gently over a low heat. Once it starts to soften, add the leeks and celery. Cook until everything is softened, then add the cider and stock, and bring to the boil.

Drop in the cauliflower and cook until soft. Gently stir in the Stilton, then season and purée with a hand blender. Once smooth, stir in the cream, mace and nutmeg.

Preheat the oven to 190°C/375°F/gas mark 5.

To make the scones, cook the potatoes until soft. Drain the potatoes and allow to cool. Sift the flour with the seasoning and baking powder into a large bowl. Add the butter and rub together until it looks like breadcrumbs. Mix in the most of the cheeses, the cooked potato, the basil (if using) and sage.

In another bowl, beat together the egg, milk and mustard. Mix the egg mixture with the cheese and potato mixture and very gently form into a rough dough.

On a lightly floured surface, roll out the dough to 2.5cm thickness. Cut into scone-sized pieces. Coat the scones with a little extra milk and top with the reserved cheese. Bake for 25 to 30 minutes.

Serve the soup with the scones and some butter.

ED'S TIP: If you don't have time to make the stock, just use a stock cube instead.

Savoury and sour vegetable soup

Although this is a Chinese dish, this style of food is so popular in Britain now that I felt we had to include a recipe for a really traditional home-cooked Chinese-style dish. I've included it in hot starters, but it could easily be bulked up and served as a main course.

SERVES 6 AS A STARTER AND 4 AS A MAIN

good handful of oyster mushrooms
1 litre vegetable stock (see page 231)
1 tablespoon freshly grated ginger
½ Chinese white cabbage, chopped into 2cm strips
1 small tin bamboo shoots, cut into long strips
1 packet rice noodles
1 small block fresh tofu, cut into long strips
2 tablespoons soy sauce
2 tablespoons (rice) vinegar
salt and freshly ground black pepper
1 egg, whisked
1 fresh red chilli, deseeded and chopped
1 spring onion, finely chopped
handful of fresh coriander, finely chopped

Pour boiling water over the oyster mushrooms and leave to soak for 20 minutes, then chop into long strips. Heat the stock in a large pan to simmering point and add the ginger, Chinese cabbage, oyster mushrooms and bamboo shoots.

Gently cook for 5 minutes. Add the noodles, cook for a further minute and then add the tofu. Add the soy sauce, vinegar and seasoning. Bring to the boil and add the egg and chilli.

Sprinkle over some spring onion and coriander. Serve in large noodle bowls.

Seasonal vegetable and bacon soup

SERVES 4

3 tablespoons olive oil
1 onion, finely chopped
2 large carrots, finely chopped
1 leek, thoroughly rinsed and finely chopped
4 rashers of streaky bacon
400g runner beans, finely chopped
1 garlic clove, chopped
4 tomatoes, finely chopped
1 teaspoon tomato purée
1 x 400g tin cannellini beans, drained
1 teaspoon dried basil
1 bay leaf
salt and freshly ground black pepper
1.2 litres vegetable stock (see page 231)
100g barley

Gently heat the olive oil in a large saucepan and add the onion, carrot, leek and bacon.

Allow to soften over a moderate heat for 3 minutes, then add the runner beans and the garlic. Allow to soften for a further 2 minutes. Now add the tomatoes and tomato purée. Cook for another minute before adding the cannellini beans, basil, bay leaf, a pinch of salt and pepper and the stock. Bring to the boil, add the barley and allow to simmer for 45 minutes.

Remove from the heat, allow to cool until warm and serve.

ED'S TIP: This soup is very good with a sprinkling of grated cheese and served with fresh tomato bread (see page 217).

Beer battered soft herring roe

SERVES 4

1 litre vegetable oil, for deep-frying

20 pairs of herring roe

salt and freshly ground black pepper

lemon wedges, to serve

FOR THE MUSTARD SAUCE

25g butter

1 tablespoon plain flour

125ml fish stock (see page 230)

125ml milk

1 teaspoon chopped fresh chives

1 teaspoon chopped fresh chervil

1 teaspoon creamed horseradish

1 teaspoon wholegrain mustard

1 teaspoon Worcestershire sauce

1 tablespoon sour cream

FOR THE BEER BATTER

2 egg whites

2 tablespoons vegetable oil

175ml porter beer

125g plain flour

FOR THE SALAD

good handful of salad leaves

small handful of chopped fresh
  parsley

small handful of chopped fresh dill

juice of ¼ lemon

olive oil

For the mustard sauce, melt the butter in a heavy saucepan. Remove from the heat and add the flour. Return to the heat and cook gently, stirring over a low heat until pale brown. Using a whisk, gradually add the stock, whisking all the time to form a smooth, silky consistency. Bring up to the boil and then allow to simmer for 2 minutes. Stir in the milk and all the other sauce ingredients, finishing with the sour cream. Take off the heat and cover with oiled greaseproof paper.

For the batter, whisk the egg whites until they have a shaving foam consistency. In a bowl, slowly mix together the oil, beer, sifted flour and a pinch of salt. Finish the batter by folding in the egg whites.

Pour the vegetable oil into a deep-sided saucepan – make sure it doesn't come any higher than halfway up the side of the pan as the level will rise once you lower in the fish. Heat the oil to 160°C/325°F using a cooking thermometer. Alternatively, drop a clove of garlic into the oil, and when it starts to fizz, the oil is at the right temperature. Remove the garlic clove.

Dip the roe into the batter and fry for 3 to 4 minutes on each side until golden brown. In a large bowl, make your salad by mixing together the salad leaves, parsley, dill, lemon juice and a touch of olive oil. Season.

Serve the roe with a large spoonful of the mustard sauce, a wedge of lemon and salad on the side.

Baked crab with ruby chard and samphire

SERVES 2

1 tablespoon olive oil

1 shallot, finely chopped

200g ruby chard, leaves separated
    and reserved, stalks finely
    chopped

good pinch of ground chilli powder

50g butter

1 tablespoon plain flour

2 tablespoons extra dry vermouth

2 tablespoons double cream

200ml semi-skimmed milk

salt and freshly ground black pepper

small bunch of parsley, finely
    chopped

100g white crab meat

3 tablespoons grated Gloucester
    cheese

FOR THE GRATIN TOPPING

1 garlic clove, chopped

½ teaspoon olive oil

knob of butter

1½ tablespoons breadcrumbs

To make the gratin topping, gently fry the garlic in oil and butter. Stir in the breadcrumbs and fry for a few minutes.

In a separate pan, heat the oil and then gently fry the shallots. Add the chard stalks. When softened, add the chilli powder and gently fry for 5 minutes.

Melt the butter in a pan and when it has melted, stir in the flour. Cook for 2 to 3 minutes, then add the vermouth and gradually stir in the cream and milk to form a rich, smooth white sauce. Cook for about 30 seconds until you have a straw-coloured roux. Season, add the parsley and chard leaves and cook gently, stirring occasionally, for 3 to 4 minutes.

Preheat the oven to 180°C/350°F/gas mark 4.

Remove the pan from the heat and add the crab meat and cheese. Pour the mixture into a buttered, ovenproof serving dish. Sprinkle over the gratin topping and bake for 10 minutes. Great served with fresh salad leaves.

Smoked mussel tart with beetroot salad

SERVES 8

40g unsalted butter

2 shallots, finely chopped

2 carrots, finely chopped

5 garlic cloves, finely chopped

bunch of fresh parsley, finely
  chopped

350ml white wine

7 egg yolks

350ml double cream

2 tins of smoked mussels

good pinch of nutmeg

good pinch of white pepper

FOR THE PASTRY

200g plain flour, plus extra for
  dusting

100g butter

pinch of salt

FOR THE SALAD

1 large shallot

1 teaspoon wine vinegar

pinch of salt

1 teaspoon mustard

pinch of sugar

4 whole cooked beetroot, cut into
  small wedges

4 tablespoons olive oil

5 anchovy fillets, thinly sliced

5 pickled walnuts, cut into small
  chunks

½ bunch of fresh flat-leaf parsley,
  leaves chopped

Start by making the pastry. Blend together the flour and butter, then add 150ml water and the salt to form a dough. Allow to rest for 30 minutes in the fridge.

Preheat the oven to 180°C/350°F/gas mark 4.

Flour a kitchen surface and roll out the pastry. Line a 25cm flan ring with the pastry. Prick the base and cover with greaseproof paper. Allow to rest for 15 minutes and then bake blind for 25 minutes. Remove from the oven and allow to cool.

Reduce the heat of the oven to 170°C/330°F/gas mark 3½.

Melt the butter in a saucepan over a low heat. Add the shallots, carrots, garlic and parsley, and allow to sweat for 15 minutes. Add the white wine, bring to the boil and reduce by three quarters.

Whilst this is reducing, beat together the egg yolks and the cream. Remove the wine, onion and parsley mixture from the heat and add the smoked mussels. Pour the egg yolk and milk mixture over the mussels, parsley, onion and wine mixture. Stir in the nutmeg and pepper. Return to a very low heat and stir gently and constantly until the mixture starts to thicken. Remove from the heat.

Place the blind-baked tart shell on to a flat baking tray. Gently ladle the thickened mixture into the tart shell and cook in the oven for 30 minutes.

Meanwhile, prepare the beetroot salad. In a bowl, mix the finely sliced shallot, vinegar, salt, mustard and sugar. Allow to sit for 10 minutes. Add the beetroot, olive oil, anchovy fillet, walnuts and parsley. Toss and serve with a slice of the mussel tart.

ED'S TIP: Use the leftover egg whites to make Eton Mess (see page 186).

British fish soup

SERVES 4

100g butter

1 leek, thoroughly rinsed and chopped

2 onions, finely chopped

4 celery stalks, finely chopped

2 carrots, finely chopped

2 fennel bulbs, finely chopped

4 garlic cloves, finely chopped

good pinch of dried red chilli

1 tablespoon tomato purée

bunch of fresh curly parsley, chopped

100g plain flour

1 orange, peeled and quartered

1 small celeriac, peeled and chopped

175ml white wine

175ml Noilly Prat (or dry vermouth)

3 star anise

1.2 litres fish stock (see page 230)

salt and white pepper

150ml cream

2 pollack fillets, cut into chunks

225g monkfish tail, cut into chunks

200g white crab meat

Melt the butter in a large saucepan. Add the leek, onions, celery, carrots, fennel, garlic and dried chilli. Cook until all the ingredients are soft.

Add the tomato purée. Cook for a further 2 minutes and stir in the parsley and flour. Cook for a further 2 minutes, then add the orange, celeriac, white wine and Noilly Prat or dry vermouth. Gently bring back to the boil and reduce by half.

Add the star anise, fish stock and a half a teaspoon each of salt and pepper. Bring to the boil, stirring occasionally. Allow to simmer for 1 hour.

Remove from the heat and allow to cool. Fish out and discard the star anise, and purée the soup in a food processor until smooth.

Place back on the heat in a saucepan. Add the cream and chunks of pollack and monkfish. Cook for 2 minutes, then stir in the crab meat and serve.

Smoked mackerel soufflé

Serve with watercress tossed in lemon and olive oil and seasoned.

SERVES 4

1 x shortcrust pastry recipe (see page 223)

1 teaspoon strong horseradish sauce

200g smoked mackerel

1 teaspoon mustard

pinch of cayenne pepper

juice of ½ lemon

salt and freshly ground pepper

4 eggs, separated

FOR THE WHITE SAUCE

25g butter

25g flour

150ml milk

150ml double cream

100g Cheddar cheese

Preheat an oven to 180°C/350°F/gas mark 4.

Roll out the pastry and line a 25cm pastry tin. Line the pastry case with greaseproof paper and baking beans. Allow to rest for 30 minutes in the fridge, then bake blind for 10 minutes. Remove and allow to cool.

To make the white sauce, melt the butter in a saucepan and stir in the flour. Cook for 2 to 3 minutes, slowly add the milk and cream.

To make the filling, mix together the horseradish, smoked mackerel, mustard, cayenne pepper, lemon juice and some salt and pepper in a bowl.

Remove the white sauce from the heat. Add the cheese and the smoked mackerel and horseradish mixture to the sauce and allow the filling to cool.

Once completely cool, fold the egg yolks through the filling mixture. Using an electric whisk, beat the egg white to form firm peaks. Now fold half the whisked egg whites into the filling. Then very gently fold the filling into the remaining egg whites. Pour this mixture into the tart shell. Bake for 20 minutes.

Goat's cheese, bean, egg and anchovy salad

This is a very simple salad that looks stunning as long as you prepare all the ingredients correctly. The contrast of all the colours really looks appetising.

SERVES 4

4 eggs

salt

250g green beans, topped and tailed

300g goat's cheese, sliced

100g anchovy fillets

FOR THE DRESSING

6 cherry tomatoes, finely chopped

pinch of sugar

½ teaspoon English mustard

1 tablespoon sherry vinegar

5 tablespoons olive oil

bunch of fresh curly parsley, finely chopped

To prepare the dressing, put the cherry tomatoes in a bowl with a pinch of salt and the sugar. Add the remaining dressing ingredients and beat together using a whisk. Pour the dressing into a clean jam jar. Screw the lid on, shake vigorously for a minute or two and then place in the fridge to chill.

Soft-boil the eggs (see tip). Carefully peel the eggs and put to one side.

At this point, prepare to assemble the salad quickly, so it's made while the beans are still hot. In a large pot of boiling, salted water, blanch the beans for 4 minutes. Drain immediately and place into a bowl. Add the cheese and mix with a spoon, then add the dressing. Finally, add the anchovy fillets.

Divide the mixture equally between four plates. Cut the soft-boiled eggs in half and place on top. Finish the dish by drizzling any dressing remaining in the bowl over the eggs.

ED'S TIP: Boil the eggs for 4 minutes if they're at room temperature, or for 4½ minutes if you've kept them in the fridge.

Crispy ham, asparagus, egg and beetroot salad

The combination of crispy, salty ham and the smooth flavour of asparagus says 'summer' to me. Wonderful with toasted walnut bread.

SERVES 4

vegetable oil

250g thinly sliced ham

bunch of English asparagus

4 ducks' eggs (or your preferred type)

200g cooked beetroot, cut into chunks

FOR THE MUSTARD DRESSING

4 tablespoons olive oil

1 teaspoon English mustard

2 teaspoons vinegar

bunch of fresh parsley, chopped

Preheat the oven to 220°C/425°F/gas mark 7. Line an oven tray with tinfoil and then lightly grease with oil.

Add the slices of ham, ensuring they do not overlap. Bake in the oven for 5 minutes or until completely crisp. Allow to cool.

Cook the asparagus for 3 minutes in boiling salted water. Strain, cut the spears in two lengthways and place to one side.

Boil the eggs for 3 minutes in salted water, then peel.

To make the mustard dressing, mix the oil, mustard and vinegar together. Stir in the chopped parsley. Place the beetroot into a bowl and pour over the dressing.

To assemble your starter, divide the dressed beetroot equally among four plates. Sprinkle over the wafers of crisp ham. Add a handful of asparagus to each plate and finish by laying a soft-boiled egg on top. Drizzle over any remaining juices from the beetroot bowl.

Green bean, bacon and tomato salad

SERVES 4

200g green beans, topped and tailed

salt and freshly ground black pepper

8 slices of smoked streaky bacon

12 vine-ripened cherry tomatoes, quartered

2 onions, finely sliced

vegetable oil

3 thick slices of country-style bread

150g good-quality Stilton cheese

small bunch of fresh tarragon, finely chopped

1 garlic clove, finely chopped

1 tablespoon white wine vinegar

1 teaspoon English mustard

pinch of sugar

Preheat the oven to 180°C/350°F/gas mark 4. Line a baking tray with tinfoil and another one with greaseproof paper.

Cook the beans in salted, boiling water for 3 or 4 minutes. Drain and keep to one side. Place the bacon on the greaseproof paper-lined tray and place in the oven for 8 minutes. Remove and set aside.

Lay the tomatoes on a plate and sprinkle lightly with salt. Fry the onions in 1 tablespoon oil over a moderate heat until pale brown in colour.

Cut the bread into large cubes, about 2 x 2cm. Place on the tinfoil-lined baking tray, drizzle over 5 tablespoons of oil, sprinkle with a good pinch of black pepper and toss. Flake over the Stilton and add the softened onions. Bake in the oven for 6 minutes. Remove and allow to cool.

Put the tarragon, garlic, vinegar, 3 tablespoons vegetable oil, the mustard and sugar into a bowl. Whisk thoroughly to make a dressing.

Combine the tomatoes with the beans, pour the dressing over them and toss. Quickly fold through the croûtons and divide evenly between four plates and top with the crispy bacon.

Butternut squash, pear and hazelnut salad

The thing I love about this salad is the fascinating combination of flavours – sweet, semi-sweet, bitter and nutty. Make sure you use good-quality, ripe pears and don't under-roast the squash.

SERVES 4

2 ripe pears, quartered and cored

juice of 1 lemon

1 whole butternut squash, cut in half lengthways and deseeded

salt and freshly ground black pepper

4 garlic cloves

4 sprigs of fresh thyme, leaves picked

6 tablespoons olive oil

200g Lancashire cheese, broken into chunks

50g hazelnuts, chopped

Preheat the oven to 180°C/350°F/gas mark 4. Line a baking tray with a piece of tinfoil.

Slice the pears thinly and place in a bowl. Squeeze over the lemon juice and mix gently.

Cut each butternut half into three wedges. Place in the baking tray with a good pinch of salt, the unpeeled garlic cloves and the thyme leaves. Drizzle over 2 tablespoons of the olive oil and mix together with your hands. Cover with another piece of foil and seal the edges. Bake in the oven for 40 to 50 minutes.

In a bowl, mix the cheese with the chopped hazelnuts.

Remove the tinfoil bag from the oven and tear open to allow to cool. Once cooled, remove the roasted pieces of squash and garlic.

Pour the lemon juice at the bottom of the bowl of pears into a separate bowl and set aside for the dressing. Peel the roasted garlic cloves and add to the lemon juice. Add the juices from the foil bag. Gently stir the remaining olive oil into this mixture to form your dressing. Finish with a pinch of black pepper and 2 tablespoons of water.

Remove the butternut squash flesh from the skins and cut into chunks. Gently mix into the hazelnuts and cheese. Divide the mixture equally on to four plates and finish with the dressing.

Chilled leek and goat's cheese soup

Leek and potato soup has to be one of my all-time favourites. It's easy to recognise the difference between a 'good un' and a 'bad un'. This goes for this chilled version too – it's all about how long you cook the leeks for and at what temperature. Serve with crusty bread.

SERVES 4

4 tablespoons vegetable oil

2 onions, finely chopped

2 garlic cloves, chopped

4 celery sticks, finely chopped

6 large leeks, sliced in half lengthways, thoroughly rinsed and green parts discarded

75ml white wine

2 litres vegetable stock (see page 231)

2 slices of good quality bread, crust removed, torn into chunks

100g Dorstone goat's cheese

2 tablespoons double cream

bunch of fresh chives, finely sliced

salt and white pepper

In a large saucepan, gently heat the vegetable oil and add the onions, garlic, celery and leeks. Cook, stirring every minute or so, until it softens into a cooked mush.

Add the wine. Gently reduce by half, then add the vegetable stock. Bring to the boil and then, over a slow, rolling boil, reduce by two thirds. This will take about 1½ hours.

At this point, add the bread and goat's cheese. Allow to cool.

Add a few ladlefuls of soup at a time to a food processor and purée each batch for at least 1 minute until smooth. Pour each batch of soup into a large bowl. Once all the soup has been puréed, stir in the cream, chives and salt and pepper to taste.

Chill in the fridge with a piece of clingfilm resting on the surface of the soup to avoid forming a skin.

Mustard-breaded ham with celeriac

The combination of celeriac and ham works brilliantly. With a wedge of cheese, some pickled onions and a chunk of good bread, it makes for a great lunchtime meal too.

SERVES 4

900g uncooked, unsmoked ham

1 onion, studded with cloves

1 carrot

1 bay leaf

2 tablespoons cider vinegar

1 teaspoon mustard powder

1 small celeriac, cut into quarters

2 tablespoons runny honey

1 tablespoon English mustard

pinch of salt

100g toasted breadcrumbs

FOR THE WALNUT DRESSING

1 tablespoon honey

½ teaspoon English mustard

25ml walnut oil

25ml vegetable oil

½ teaspoon sugar

1 tablespoon cider vinegar

small bunch of fresh chives, finely chopped

Place the ham, onion, carrot, bay leaf, vinegar and mustard powder into a pot. Pour in 1.8 litres water, bring to a gentle boil and poach the ham for 40 minutes. Add the celeriac to the pot and cook for a further 30 minutes. Remove from the heat and allow to cool in the cooking stock.

Remove the ham, carrot and onion and place on a plate and put into the fridge to chill. Remove the celeriac and slice as thinly as possible.

Now mix together the honey and mustard with the salt. Remove the cold ham from the fridge and brush this mixture all over the ham. Take a large sheet of clingfilm and spread the breadcrumbs over it. Roll the ham in this mixture, then secure each end of the clingfilm tightly round the ham and put the parcel in the fridge.

To prepare the walnut dressing, mix the honey and mustard in a bowl. Whisk steadily, adding the walnut and vegetable oils. This should emulsify to make a thick and rich dressing. Now add the sugar and vinegar, and finish with the chives. Toss the sliced celeriac through the dressing.

Remove the ham from the fridge and slice. Cut the cooked carrot into long sticks and cut the onion (remove the cloves) into wedges. Garnish the ham and celeriac with carrot and onion and drizzle over any remaining dressing. Serve with a mound of celeriac.

Mushroom salad with quails' eggs and asparagus

I've put a British twist on a modern Spanish recipe shown to me by a trainee of the celebrated chef Ferran Adrià. Although fascinating, I found the original recipe too complicated. I've simplified it but still retained the wonderful balance of flavours.

SERVES 4

3 tablespoons vegetable oil

2 large shallots, finely chopped

200g field mushrooms, thinly sliced

100g mixed wild mushrooms, wiped and cut into small pieces

2 garlic cloves, finely chopped

12 quails' eggs

bunch of asparagus, trimmed of the woody part

salt

100g Cheshire cheese, shaved

FOR THE WHITE TRUFFLE DRESSING

100ml olive oil

1 teaspoon sherry vinegar

2 tablespoons white truffle oil

good pinch of celery salt

small bunch of fresh curly parsley, chopped

½ teaspoon English mustard

In a large pan, heat the vegetable oil. Add the finely chopped shallots, mushrooms and garlic. Fry the mushrooms vigorously over a medium-high heat until coloured. Remove from the heat and allow to steep in the pan until cool. Place a sieve over a saucepan and pour the mushrooms through the sieve to collect the juices. Evenly spread the mushrooms out over four plates, laying them flat.

Set a timer to 2 minutes and 16 seconds and soft-boil the eggs. Once boiled, lightly crack the shell of the eggs all over. Hold the eggs, one by one, under gently running water while very carefully peeling them.

To make the dressing, bring the oil and mushroom juice up to a gentle boil, then whisk in the sherry vinegar, white truffle oil, celery salt and chopped parsley. Remove from the heat, continue whisking and add in the mustard.

Cut each asparagus spear in half lengthways. Blanch in boiling salted water for 3 minutes. Strain and add the asparagus spears to the dressing while hot.

Arrange the dressed asparagus spears over the warm mushrooms. Now add the whole, soft-boiled quail's eggs, three per plate.

Top with shavings of cheese and a drizzle of remaining dressing.

Bass with lime, salt and chilli

The inspiration for this recipe came from Ernest Hemingway's *The Old Man and the Sea*. On board the boat, the Cuban fisherman would eat mackerel with salt and lime as a snack. I did a similar thing down in Swanage with a line-caught bass. In the height of summer, this is a lovely and refreshing dish. Savour with a glass of chilled, crisp white wine.

SERVES 4
450g bass fillet (skinned and
  pinboned)
2 fresh red chillies, deseeded and
  sliced
¼ teaspoon chilli powder
1 large shallot, very finely sliced
salt
juice of 2 limes
small bunch of fresh flat-leaf parsley,
  leaves roughly chopped
50ml vegetable oil
50g jar of salmon eggs

With a sharp knife, slice the raw bass fillet as thinly as you can across the flesh to create long, thin slices similar to smoked salmon.

In a bowl, combine the chilli, shallot, a pinch of salt and the lime juice. Allow this to steep for 30 minutes, then add the parsley leaves and oil.

Liberally spoon this mixture over the raw bass fillets. Chill on plates in the fridge for 1 hour.

To serve, spoon 1 teaspoon of salmon eggs on to each plate. By now, the lime juice will have reacted with the raw bass and 'cooked' it.

Potted crab

Ideally, you should buy a live crab and cook it yourself (see tip). If using a live crab, you need a 900g crab to get 225g crab meat. But if you have neither the time nor the inclination, this is one of the few recipes that could lend itself to either dressed or even tinned crab meat.

SERVES 4
100g butter
3 egg yolks
225g white and brown crab meat
juice of 1 lemon
30ml cream
1 tablespoon chopped fresh chervil
pinch of cayenne pepper
1 teaspoon seed mustard
salt and freshly ground black pepper
slices of white bread, toasted

Melt 25g butter and lightly brush it around the inside of four espresso cups. Place in the fridge to allow the butter to harden.

Beat the egg yolks until light and fluffy, then stir in the crab meat and lemon juice.

In a saucepan, gently melt the remaining butter with the cream over a low heat. Stir in the crab with the chervil, cayenne, mustard and a pinch of salt and pepper.

Warm through but do not allow to boil as this will make the eggs curdle. Remove from the heat and allow to cool. Firmly push the mixture into the four espresso cups and chill, ideally overnight.

To serve, plunge each cup into scalding hot water, turn out on to a plate and serve with white toast.

ED'S TIP: To cook a live crab, drop it in boiling, salted water and cook for 8 minutes. Drain in a colander and allow to cool. Do not hold under running water to make it cool faster. Once cool, crack the shell with a hammer and pick out the meat.

Trout and horseradish mousse

The combination of trout and horseradish is a classic. This dish is a great dinner party starter – once made you can place it in the fridge to then focus on creating your main course.

SERVES 4

butter, for greasing
2 bay leaves
1 small onion, finely chopped
1 carrot, finely chopped
1 teaspoon peppercorns
1 teaspoon vinegar
2 x 300g trout fillets
2 egg yolks
200g cream cheese
juice of 2 lemons
1 tablespoon creamed horseradish
pinch of cayenne pepper
salt
4 slices of sourdough bread, toasted
handful of mixed salad leaves

FOR THE SMOKED SALMON AND CAPER DRESSING

1 teaspoon capers, chopped
200g smoked salmon, finely chopped
juice of 1 lemon
4 anchovy fillets
small bunch of fresh dill
1 tablespoon cream
pinch of cayenne pepper

Preheat the oven to 180°C/350°F/gas mark 4. Grease four small ramekins with butter.

Put the bay leaves, onion, carrot, peppercorns and vinegar into a large frying pan. Add 2 litres water and place on the heat. Gently poach the trout fillets in the water for 6 minutes. Remove from the heat and allow to cool, then skin the fillets.

Place the egg yolks, cream cheese and lemon juice into a blender and whiz together. Add one of the trout fillets to the blender. Whiz for 30 seconds to form a smooth mousse. Spoon into a bowl. Flake the second trout fillet into the mousse. Stir in the horseradish, cayenne pepper and a pinch of salt.

Spoon the mixture into the ramekins. Wrap in tinfoil and place on to a deep oven tray. Pour enough water into the oven tray to come one third of the way up the sides of the ramekins. Cook in the oven for 15 minutes.

For the dressing, combine the capers with the smoked salmon, lemon juice, anchovy fillets and dill. Stir in the cream and a pinch of cayenne pepper.

Remove the trout mousses from the oven and allow to cool. Turn each one out on to a plate. Spoon over some of the dressing and serve with the sourdough bread and a handful of mixed leaves.

Grilled sardines with eggs and kale

In the warmer waters of the West Country, sardines are in abundance and easy to catch, although here in Britain we often call them pilchards – I don't know why. But sardines have a slightly more romantic sound, so I'm sticking with that for this recipe. Enjoy them with toasted sourdough or cornbread.

SERVES 4

8 medium-sized sardines

1 tablespoon olive oil

4 eggs

200g kale, washed thoroughly

salt

FOR THE DRESSING

bunch of fresh mint, leaves picked

1 red onion, sliced

2 small shallots, sliced

½ teaspoon wholegrain mustard

2 tablespoons red wine vinegar

Prepare the sardines by splitting open the bellies and rinsing out the inside. Alternatively, ask your fishmonger to gut the fish for you. Place each cleaned sardine on a chopping board, belly down. Using the back of your hand, squash the sardine flat to loosen the spine. Turn it over and, with scissors, snip the spine away from the head.

Heat the olive oil in a frying pan over a moderate heat and then slowly cook the sardines, skin side down, for around 5 minutes. Remove the pan from the heat, turn the sardines over and allow them to rest in the cooling pan for 10 minutes.

Meanwhile, mix together the dressing ingredients. Allow to steep.

Soft-boil the eggs for 4½ minutes. Boil the kale in salted water for 5 minutes and strain. Allow to cool but do not rinse.

Add the dressing to the kale and mix thoroughly.

Place equal amounts of kale on each plate. Turn over the sardines and remove the central bone and any of the hair bones. Lay next to the portion of kale. Add the soft-boiled eggs and finish with any leftover dressing.

ED'S TIP: I always like to use Burford Brown eggs as they have very rich yolks.

Lobster cocktail

SERVES 4
1 x 750g live lobster
salt
250ml white truffle oil
2 egg yolks
1 lemon, cut into wedges
4 plum tomatoes
bunch of fresh basil, leaves finely
    sliced
4 tablespoons olive oil
½ teaspoon sherry vinegar
1 avocado, peeled, stoned and cut
    into small cubes
bunch of fresh chives, finely chopped
mayonnaise
4 thin slices of good bread, toasted
    (walnut bread is great for this)

Kill the lobster by driving a knife down into the cross mark on its head. Cook it in boiling salted water for 10 minutes. Allow to cool, then cut in half lengthways. Remove the white meat from the claws and the tail. Finely slice the tail meat. Keep the claws whole.

Gently whisk the truffle oil into the egg yolks, then add a teaspoon of lemon juice and a pinch of salt. Score the tomatoes with an 'x' on their bottoms. Immerse in boiling water for 10 seconds before dunking them in iced water. Peel and discard the skins.

Quarter the tomatoes and remove the seeds, then finely chop the tomato flesh. Place in a bowl and mix in the basil, olive oil and sherry vinegar.

Finally, mix the avocado cubes with the lobster meat. Add the chives and a little mayonnaise to bind. To serve, spoon the lobster mixture into pretty cocktail glasses. Top with the truffle oil mixture, tomato salsa and finish a thin slice of bread. Serve with a wedge of lemon.

Pressed ham hock

Enjoy the ham with an onion marmalade and toasted country bread.

SERVES 10
3 ham hocks
1 bay leaf
1 onion, studded with cloves
2 leeks, thoroughly rinsed
2 carrots
½ teaspoon salt
½ teaspoon black pepper
1 teaspoon powdered English mustard
bunch of fresh curly parsley, chopped
1 tablespoon olive oil

Place all the ingredients except the parsley and olive oil into a large 3-litre casserole. Pour in 1.2 litres of water. Bring to the boil and cook gently for 3 hours. Allow to cool, gently lift out all the cooked vegetables and set aside.

Remove the ham hocks and place in a bowl. Strain the liquid into a saucepan and reduce by three quarters over a high heat. Carefully remove the meat from the bones and place the meat into a bowl, mixing with the parsley.

Lightly brush the edges of a large terrine mould with the olive oil. Add the reserved vegetables to the ham, pour in the reduced liquid and mix. Spoon into the mould, filling it right to the top. Cover with clingfilm and press down with a weight. Chill for at least 4 hours.

Slice and serve.

Beef Wellington with red wine gravy

Rumour has it that the famous General Wellington, whilst busy defeating Napoleon, acquired and enjoyed French cooking skills, but so as not to offend or demoralise his men, he combined the delicacies of French puff pastry with the British obsession for eating beef. I've chosen to use English rough puff pastry as I imagine on the battle field it would be almost impossible to produce perfect puff pastry! Also, I prefer the contrasting textures you get when you use rough puff pastry.

SERVES 4

beef dripping or vegetable oil

salt and freshly ground black pepper

375g Scottish beef fillet

3 large shallots, chopped

10 button mushrooms, chopped

sprig of fresh thyme, leaves finely
  chopped

2 slices of brown bread, made into
  breadcrumbs

½ glass of red wine

flour, for dusting

1 x rough puff pastry recipe (see
  page 226)

1 teaspoon English mustard

1 egg, beaten

FOR THE RED WINE GRAVY

600ml beef stock (see page 230)

25g butter

1 glass of red wine

Heat a little beef dripping or oil in a frying pan. Season the beef fillet then seal on all sides in the hot pan until nut-brown. Remove the beef from pan and set aside.

Fry the shallots and mushrooms in oil with the thyme. Add the breadcrumbs and cook for another 30 seconds, then add the red wine. Cook until it thickens then finely chop to create a mushroom pâté. Allow to cool.

Preheat the oven to 200°C/400°F/gas mark 6. Grease a roasting tray with a little oil.

On a floured working surface, roll out the pastry to a rectangular shape large enough to enclose the beef fillet – about triple the width of the fillet and one and a half times the length. Spread with the mustard, cover with the cooled mushroom pâté and place the beef along the bottom edge of the rolled-out pastry. Roll the beef with the pastry to cover. Seal the edges, folding the ends together to keep the juices in. Brush with beaten egg and slide on to the greased tray. Refrigerate for at least 1 hour.

Roast the Wellington in the oven until the pastry is golden. This will take about 20 to 30 minutes.

Meanwhile, to make the red wine gravy, pour the stock into a saucepan and reduce on a high heat by three quarters. Add the butter and whisk vigorously. Place the red wine into a separate saucepan and also reduce by three quarters. Whisk the reduced wine into the stock and butter mixture.

To serve, cut the beef so that you can see the pink of the meat and serve with fresh seasonal vegetables. My personal favourite with beef Wellington is boiled and buttered Savoy cabbage.

Beef with Jimmy McCurry sauce

Traditionally the belly of a cow is used as stewing steak in Britain. However, in South America it is prized as a great grilling steak. Not only is it very affordable but it's absolutely delicious too, as long as you cook it to medium rare or medium only. Any longer than that and it becomes extremely tough. It's also vital to let the meat rest before tucking in.

In Argentina, the marinade I use is known as chimichurri. It is believed the unusual name comes from the name Jimmy McCurry, an Irishman who is said to have introduced the marinade when marching with General Belgrano in the nineteenth century. It became a popular way to prepare beef, and the recipe was passed on. However, Jimmy McCurry was difficult for the natives to pronounce and became chimichurri!

SERVES 2

2 x 250g skirt steaks
2 eggs, beaten
200ml milk
1 large Spanish onion, thinly sliced
75g plain flour
vegetable oil

FOR THE JIMMY MCCURRY SAUCE

200g large red peppers
olive oil
salt and freshly ground black pepper
8 garlic cloves, chopped
bunch of fresh flat-leaf parsley,
  leaves picked and chopped
4 tablespoons sherry vinegar
2 tablespoons lemon juice

FOR THE BEEF MARINADE

pinch of dried chilli flakes
½ teaspoon sugar
1 tablespoon red wine vinegar
½ tablespoon finely chopped fresh
  thyme
zest and juice of ½ lime

Preheat the oven to 220°C/425°F/gas mark 7.

Toss the whole peppers in olive oil and salt then bake in the oven for 30 to 40 minutes until dark on all sides. Remove from the oven, place in a bowl, cover with clingfilm and allow to cool. Once cooled, remove the skin and seeds and roughly chop.

Now make the Jimmy McCurry sauce. Combine the chopped peppers, chopped garlic, parsley, vinegar and lemon juice with 4 tablespoons of olive oil, 1 teaspoon of salt and ½ teaspoon of freshly ground black pepper. Mix well, then pulse in a food processor or mix in a pestle and mortar, but do not purée. Taste and adjust the seasoning if necessary. Allow to stand for at least 2 hours.

Mix all the beef marinade ingredients and 4 tablespoons vegetable oil together in a bowl. Place the steaks in the bowl, mix with the marinade, cover and refrigerate for at least 2 hours.

Whisk together the eggs and milk. Toss in the sliced onion and leave to stand for 30 minutes, stirring occasionally.

Place the flour in a large bowl and season with salt and pepper. Pour vegetable oil into a deep frying pan to a depth of 2.5cm. Place over a high heat. Lift the onions out of the egg mixture with a slotted spoon and toss them in the flour. Fry, in batches, in the oil until golden brown and drain on kitchen paper.

Remove the beef from the marinade. Heat a frying pan or griddle pan and cook the steaks quickly for 2 to 3 minutes on each side.

To serve, place the hot steaks on individual plates and top with McCurry sauce. Serve with the fried onions.

ED'S TIP: Jimmy McCurry sauce, covered and kept in the fridge, will last for several days, although the flavours will weaken a little over time.

Braised shin of beef
with green peppercorns

It is essential that beef shin is slow-cooked. It's usually sold as braising steak, but you're best off asking your butcher for beef shin on the bone, cut into two pieces. Each piece will feed at least four people. Supermarkets usually use this cut to make extra lean mince.

SERVES UP TO 8

8 tablespoons flour

1 teaspoon nutmeg

¼ teaspoon cinnamon

½ teaspoon celery salt

1 teaspoon white pepper

1 beef shin, cut into 2 pieces

100g beef dripping

250ml Madeira

250ml red wine

500ml beef stock (see page 230)

4 carrots, roughly chopped

4 small onions, roughly chopped

1 head of celery, roughly chopped

100g butter

1 small tin or jar green peppercorns, drained

sprig of fresh thyme

4 bay leaves

Preheat the oven to 160°C/325°F/gas mark 3.

Place a large casserole pot, or two smaller pots, on to a medium heat. Combine the flour, spices, celery salt and white pepper and liberally dust the beef with this mixture.

Add the dripping to the casserole pot and seal the beef shins on all sides until dark brown in colour. Remove the meat from the pot and set aside.

Pour the Madeira and wine into the pot, bring up to the boil and reduce the liquid by half, scraping any sediment from the bottom. Add the liquid to the beef stock, skimming off any fat that rises to the surface.

Place the empty casserole pot back on the heat and add the carrots, onions, celery and butter. Cook over a moderate heat for 3 to 4 minutes then add the peppercorns, a good sprig of thyme, the bay leaves and the alcohol-flavoured stock. Lower the sealed beef shins into the liquid. Bring to a gentle boil, then take off the heat, cover with greaseproof paper and a lid and place in the oven.

After 1 hour, turn the heat down to 150°C/300°F/ gas mark 2 and cook for a further 2½ hours. Turn the oven off and leave the beef in the oven to rest for at least 30 minutes.

Remove the pot from the oven and place back on the hob. Very carefully lift out the beef shins, allowing all the juices to drain back into the cooking liquid. Place on to a large tray. Using a slotted spoon, remove all the vegetables and herbs to the tray. Vigorously boil down the remaining juices by two thirds. Once they have been reduced, add the beef and vegetables back to the rich liquid. Cover and heat through for 10 minutes.

ED'S TIP: This is ideal with fluffy mash. I find it best to remove the meat from the bone by ripping it using kitchen tongs, laying it over the mash and ladling over the vegetables with some sauce.

Beef stew with
blue cheese dumplings

For me this has to be the ultimate 'one-pot' experience. The combination of braised beef brisket with Stilton and walnut dumplings is sensational. Lovely with crusty bread.

SERVES 4

½ teaspoon ground mace

½ teaspoon ground black pepper

½ teaspoon salt

2 tablespoons plain flour

1kg beef brisket, cut into chunks

5 tablespoons beef dripping or
   vegetable oil

100g butter

2 medium onions, cut into 1cm cubes

4 medium carrots, cut into 1cm cubes

200g chestnut mushrooms, quartered

6 garlic cloves (use smoked garlic if
   available)

bunch of fresh curly parsley, finely
   chopped

400ml English ale

2 litres beef stock (see page 230)

2 bay leaves

FOR THE DUMPLINGS

250g self-raising flour

125g suet, shredded

¼ teaspoon salt

150g Stilton cheese, crumbled

50g ground walnuts

Mix the mace, pepper and salt with the flour. Dust the chunks of beef in the seasoned flour, reserving the leftover flour. In a large casserole pot, heat 3 tablespoons of the beef dripping or oil and half the butter over a moderate heat. Add the beef to the hot fat and seal and colour on all sides until nut brown. Remove the meat from the dish and place on a large plate to cool. Allow the casserole dish to cool.

Place the onions, carrots, mushrooms and garlic into the cooled casserole dish. Add the remaining butter and put back on a moderate heat. Cook gently, stirring constantly, for 3 minutes. Now stir through half the parsley and the reserved flour. Cook for a further 2 minutes. Pour in the ale, bring to the boil and add the beef stock and bay leaves. Stir and scrape the sediment from the bottom of the casserole dish. Once the liquid has come to the boil, turn to the lowest heat, add the beef and cook very gently for 50 minutes.

Once the stew is cooking, make the dumplings. Sift the flour into a large bowl. Add the suet, the remaining parsley and ¼ teaspoon of salt. Gently add the chunks of stilton and the ground walnuts. Using your fingertips, start to work this to form a dough. Only use your fingertips, otherwise your dumplings will become gelatinous. Form the dumplings into large marble-sized balls and place on to greaseproof paper. Once all the dumplings have been prepared, add them to the casserole pot using a slotted spoon and cook for 40 minutes.

Serve the beef stew and dumplings in deep-sided bowls.

ED'S TIP: To keep the dumplings fluffy and light, your stew must not boil. It is important to make the dumplings only just before cooking them.

Meat and tatties, R&A style

R&A stands for Randall & Aubin, my restaurant in London's Soho. This is a meal that I'll often make for myself in the restaurant when I've forgotten to eat during a busy shift and suddenly find myself completely starving. Delicious.

SERVES 2

1 tin anchovies

4 sprigs of fresh rosemary, leaves
  picked

100g softened butter, plus an extra
  knob

zest and juice of 1 lemon

4 field mushrooms, sliced

2 garlic cloves, crushed

½ teaspoon sugar

salt and freshly ground black pepper

3 medium King Edward potatoes,
  peeled and cut into 5cm chunks

½ teaspoon chilli powder

olive oil

2 shallots, finely sliced

2 x 275g rib eye steaks

1 teaspoon celery salt

Drain the anchovies, then place into a pestle and mortar and grind to a paste with the rosemary leaves. Mix with the softened butter and incorporate half the lemon zest and juice.

Fry the mushrooms and garlic gently in the anchovy butter for 15 minutes. Add the remaining lemon juice and the sugar and season.

Cook the potatoes in boiling water for 6 minutes. Drain and pat dry. Sprinkle with a pinch of salt and the chilli powder. Heat the knob of butter with some olive oil in a pan and pan-fry the potatoes over a moderate heat until lightly golden. Add the shallots and fry until softened. Drain on kitchen paper.

Heat a griddle pan. Coat the steaks each in 1 teaspoon olive oil and the celery salt and griddle to your liking. Serve the steaks with the potatoes and the mushrooms.

Slow-cooked shin of veal

SERVES 6

3kg veal shin

seasoned flour, for dusting

olive oil

100g butter

2 carrots, finely chopped

4 celery sticks, finely chopped

1 onion, finely chopped

1 red pepper, finely chopped

2 fresh red chillies, finely chopped

6 garlic cloves, chopped

10 anchovy fillets

2 x 400g tins peeled tomatoes

1 bottle of dry white wine

bunch of fresh curly parsley, finely
  chopped

bunch of fresh thyme, leaves picked
  and finely chopped

zest and juice of 1 lemon

Preheat the oven to 150°C/300°F/gas mark 2.

Dust the veal in seasoned flour. Heat 50ml olive oil in a large deep-sided pot and fry the veal until golden. Remove and set aside.

Melt the butter in the same pan, add 4 more tablespoons of olive oil and fry the vegetables, chilli and garlic until soft. Add the anchovies and cook for a further minute. Now add the tinned tomatoes, wine, parsley and thyme and cook for a further 10 minutes.

Place the veal into a deep-sided casserole, pour the sauce over top, add the lemon zest and juice and cover with foil. Cook in the oven for 1 hour then reduce the temperature to 120°C/250°F/gas mark ½ and cook for a further 2 hours.

Remove from the oven and serve.

ED'S TIP: This goes well with mashed potatoes, pan-fried spinach and a sprinkle of chopped parsley and lemon zest.

Roast rib of beef with Yorkshire puddings

SERVES 4

500g King Edward potatoes, peeled
  and chopped
salt and freshly ground black pepper
150g goose fat
vegetable oil
2-rib beef joint
bunch of fresh thyme, leaves chopped
1 teaspoon mustard powder
2 carrots, chopped
2 celery sticks, chopped
3 red onions, chopped
750ml beef stock (see page 230)

FOR THE HORSERADISH SAUCE

15g fresh horseradish, grated
1 tablespoon white wine vinegar
150ml double cream
pinch of caster sugar
pinch of English mustard powder
dash of fresh lemon juice

FOR THE YORKSHIRE PUDDINGS

4 eggs
150ml semi-skimmed milk
250g plain flour
50g beef dripping or 4 tablespoons
  vegetable oil

Preheat the oven to 220°C/425°F/gas mark 7.

Parboil the potatoes in salted water for 10 minutes, then drain. Place a roasting tray, with the goose fat in it, in the oven to heat up.

Heat a second roasting tray on the hob with some oil. Rub some black pepper into the beef and seal in the roasting tray. Sprinkle with the thyme and mustard powder. Place the chopped carrots, celery and onion in the roasting tin with the beef on top, fat side up.

When the goose fat is hot, remove the tray from the oven and add the potatoes to the tray, spooning over the fat and sprinkling with salt.

Place both the potato tray and the beef tray in the oven, the beef above the potatoes, and roast for 10 minutes, then reduce the heat to 180°C/350°F/gas mark 4 and cook for a further 30 minutes.

Meanwhile, make the horseradish sauce. Mix the horseradish and vinegar in a bowl. Add the cream, sugar, mustard and lemon juice to the horseradish mixture and season. Mix well.

For the Yorkshire puddings, whisk together the eggs, milk and 150ml cold water in a bowl and leave to rest for 15 minutes. Sieve the flour into the mixture, mix well and season.

Remove the beef from the oven, cover with tinfoil and allow to rest for 20 minutes while the potatoes continue to roast.

Grease a 8-hole Yorkshire pudding tin with the beef dripping or oil. Put in the oven to heat up for 5 minutes. When the dripping is hot, spoon enough Yorkshire pudding batter into each hole to fill it halfway up, and return to the oven for 20 minutes.

Remove the vegetables from the beef tray and set aside. Skim off the fat from the juices in the tray. Heat the tray on the hob, add the beef stock and the reserved vegetables. Reduce by half and then strain the gravy into a jug.

Carve the beef. Remove the Yorkshire puddings and potatoes from the oven. Arrange on individual plates, spoon the gravy over and serve the horseradish on the side.

ED'S TIP: I would serve this with some boiled seasonal vegetables.

Roast beef fillet with plum sauce

Although this is a rather expensive recipe to produce, it's worth putting together for a big occasion or hot buffet-style lunch. Ketjap manis, a thick sweet soy sauce, although not readily available in every grocers, can be sourced relatively easily.

SERVES 4

1.2kg beef fillet

salt

1 teaspoon Szechuan pepper

20 new potatoes, halved

olive oil

1 tablespoon soy sauce

400g green beans, topped and tailed

1 lime

4 plums, stoned and halved

FOR THE MARINADE

1 tablespoon light soy sauce

1 tablespoon ketjap manis

1 tablespoon rice wine

4 garlic cloves, finely chopped

Make the marinade by mixing together the soy sauce, ketjap manis, rice wine, garlic and ½ teaspoon Szechuan pepper in a large bowl. Add the beef and leave to marinate for an hour or so in the fridge.

Preheat the oven to 200°C/400°F/gas mark 6. Line a baking tray with tinfoil.

Bring a pan of salted water to the boil. Blanch the potatoes for 6 minutes, then drain them and toss in 2 tablespoons olive oil and ½ teaspoon of Szechuan pepper. Pop in the oven and roast for 20 minutes until crispy. Toss in the soy sauce and roast for more 5 minutes until caramelised. Keep warm.

Meanwhile, heat a frying pan until hot then pour in 1 tablespoon olive oil. Remove the beef from the marinade and sear all over in the hot pan.

Transfer to the lined baking tray, pour over the remaining marinade and cover with tinfoil. Place in the oven with the potatoes and roast for 8 minutes. Remove the top layer of foil and roast for a further 3 minutes.

Boil the green beans and strain. Finish the potatoes with a squeeze of lime.

Remove the beef from the oven and set aside to rest. Pour the juices from the tray into a frying pan, add the plums and simmer for 5 minutes or until the plums are softened.

To serve, carve the beef into thick slices and place on a serving plate. Drizzle over the plum sauce and serve with the potatoes and beans.

Ham with colcannon and mustard sauce

SERVES 4

1kg salt-cured ham

1 Savoy cabbage

2 bay leaves

1 teaspoon black peppercorns

bunch of fresh parsley

3 garlic cloves

1 onion, quartered

1 teaspoon mustard powder

1 teaspoon red wine vinegar

salt and freshly ground black pepper

500g Vivaldi or Maris Piper potatoes, peeled and quartered

50g butter

1 teaspoon vegetable oil

bunch of spring onions, finely sliced

100ml milk

pinch of nutmeg

100ml single cream

FOR THE WHITE SAUCE

75g butter

50g plain flour

200ml medium-sweet cider

1 bay leaf

1 tablespoon wholegrain mustard

100ml single cream

Rinse the ham in a bowl under running water for 5 minutes. Remove the outer leaves from the cabbage. Shred the inner leaves and put to one side. Cut the outer leaves into strips.

Pour 1.5 litres of water into a saucepan and add the strips of outer cabbage leaves, bay leaves, peppercorns, most of the parsley, the garlic, onion, mustard powder and vinegar. Bring to the boil, then add the ham and cover with a lid. Turn the heat right down and allow to cook gently for 2 hours.

After 1 hour, bring a new pan of salted water to the boil. Add the potatoes and cook until soft.

In a saucepan, heat the butter and oil for the colcannon and fry the shredded cabbage. Once it starts to soften, add the spring onions, milk, nutmeg and some salt and pepper. Bring to the boil and simmer gently for 5 minutes. Remove from the heat.

Drain the potatoes, lightly dry them in a pan over a moderate heat and mash. Gradually add the milky cabbage mixture, stirring to avoid lumps. Put aside.

For the white sauce, melt the butter gently in a saucepan. Add the flour and stir constantly until the mixture is straw coloured. Remove from the heat.

When the ham is cooked, drain off the cooking liquid through a sieve over a jug. Set the cooking liquid aside. Place the flour mixture back on the heat and slowly add the cider and 1 litre of the cooking liquid, stirring constantly. If any lumps form, use a whisk. Add the bay leaf, then cook over a gentle heat for 15 minutes.

Finely chop the remaining parsley and add to the sauce. Check for seasoning, and finally add the wholegrain mustard and the cream. Keep warm over a gentle heat.

Warm the colcannon and finish with the cream. Check the seasoning and add more salt, pepper and nutmeg if required.

To serve, spoon the colcannon on to individual plates. Slice the ham into 1cm slices and place over the colcannon and finish with a ladle of sauce over the top.

Slow-cooked pork belly with pork crackling

I have based this recipe on the winning recipe of *Britain's Best Dish* in 2007. Its origins are a famous Italian recipe known as *porchetta*. I have slightly tweaked it as, like all cooks, I like to put a slight twist on recipes to make them my own. I have to say that John Kenny's version was pretty exceptional and a worthy winner of the TV show.

After winning the competition and a bucket-load of money, I asked him what he was going to do with it. He looked at me in stunned amazement and told me, 'pigs, of course'. He is a farmer with real integrity. If you want to buy some very special pork, go to John's website, www.happyhogsfarm.co.uk.

SERVES 6–8

1.8kg pork belly
bunch of fresh rosemary, leaves
    chopped
bunch of fresh sage, leaves chopped
4 garlic cloves, chopped
salt and freshly ground black pepper
1.3kg potatoes, such as Maris Piper,
    peeled and diced
butter, to taste
50ml milk
1 spring or Savoy cabbage, sliced

FOR THE SAUCE

1 banana shallot, finely chopped
300ml Norfolk cider
1 litre chicken stock (see page 230),
    warm
1 teaspoon tomato purée

FOR THE ROASTED APPLES

2 Cox's apples, halved and cored
2 large knobs of butter
1 tablespoon brown sugar
4 pinches of ground cinnamon

Preheat the oven to 220ºC/425ºF/gas mark 7.

Trim off the excess fat on the underside of the pork, then spread the pork meat with the chopped herbs and garlic. Roll and tie the pork. Pour some water into a roasting tin, place a rack on top and put the pork on the rack. Roast in the oven for 20 to 30 minutes until the pork starts to crisp up, then turn the heat down to 150ºC/300ºF/gas mark 2 and cook for about 2 hours.

Meanwhile, make the sauce. Place the shallot and cider into a saucepan and simmer for about 15 minutes until the liquid is reduced by half. Add the warm chicken stock and the tomato purée and simmer for 2 hours.

To roast the apples, place them, cut side down, in a frying pan with the butter and brown sugar. Cook until the apples start to caramelise then place them, cut side up, in a roasting tray. Sprinkle with the cinnamon, place in the oven with the pork and roast for 10 to 15 minutes. Keep warm.

Put the potatoes in a pan of salted cold water. Bring to the boil and simmer until cooked – this will take about 15 minutes. Drain and mash or pass through a potato ricer. Blend with the butter and milk until the right consistency is achieved. Season and keep warm.

Cook the cabbage in a pan of boiling water for 10 minutes, then drain. Set aside and keep warm.

When the pork is ready, remove it from the oven and allow to rest, then slice.

To serve, place a mound of mashed potato in the centre of each plate, add the cabbage and the sliced pork. Serve with roast apples and the sauce.

Spiced Caribbean pork chops

SERVES 4

4 pork chops

vegetable oil

1 onion, chopped

1 red chilli, halved lengthways

4 garlic cloves, 2 whole and 2 finely
    chopped

1 x 400g tin kidney beans

2 cups white rice

bunch of spring onions, chopped

4 tablespoons freshly grated coconut

juice of 1 lime

apple sauce, to serve

FOR THE GUAVA JELLY GRAVY

1 tablespoon guava jelly

3 tablespoons rum

400ml chicken stock (see page 230)

FOR THE SOUTHERN SPICE MIX

2 pinches of salt

2 pinches of pepper

½ teaspoon garlic powder

½ teaspoon chilli powder

½ teaspoon ground coriander

½ teaspoon ground cumin

½ teaspoon chilli flakes

½ teaspoon sugar

½ teaspoon dried onion

½ teaspoon dried mixed herbs

½ teaspoon ground nutmeg

4 tablespoons flour

Preheat the oven to 180°C/350°F/gas mark 4.

Mix all the ingredients for the southern spice mix together. Weigh out 15g of spice mix (or use half a pot of shop-bought jerk seasoning mix). Score the fatty skin of the pork chops and dust all over with the spice mix.

Grease a baking tray with a little oil, place the pork chops on the tray and bake in the oven for 25 to 30 minutes.

To make the gravy, put the guava jelly, rum and half the chicken stock in a small pan. Place over a low heat and stir until the jelly has dissolved. Set aside.

Gently fry the onion, red chilli and chopped garlic until softened. Add the beans and the remaining chicken stock and simmer for 20 minutes.

Boil the rice in 4 cups of water on a low heat until all the water has been absorbed. Add the rice to the slow-cooked beans and stir in the spring onions, grated coconut and lime juice.

Remove the pork chops from the oven, lift out of the tray and set aside to rest. Pour the juices from the tray over the rice and bean mixture and stir.

Place the rice and beans on a serving dish. Slice the pork chops and put on top of the rice and beans. Spoon over the guava jelly gravy and serve with a spoonful of apple sauce.

Chinese roast pork neck

SERVES 4

1kg pork neck, cut into 5 thick slices

4 pak choi

groundnut oil

juice of ½ lemon

1 tablespoon soy sauce

chopped spring onion, to serve

FOR THE MARINADE

100g fresh ginger, peeled and finely
   diced

10 garlic cloves, peeled and finely
   diced

3 tablespoons white sugar

2 tablespoons Chinese or malt
   vinegar

200ml dry sherry

200ml char siu or hoisin sauce

200ml Chinese barbecue sauce or
   plum sauce

1 teaspoon sesame oil

Combine the marinade ingredients in a large bowl. Add the pork and stir to coat in the marinade. Cover and leave to marinate in the fridge overnight.

The next day, preheat the oven to 190°C/375°F/ gas mark 5. Remove the pork from the bowl, reserving the marinade. Fill a deep roasting tin with 4cm water, place a wire rack inside and place the pork on top. Roast in the oven for 15 minutes, then turn the meat over and baste with generous amounts of the reserved marinade. Roast for a further 15 minutes, then baste again.

Turn the oven up to 220°C/425°F/gas mark 7 and roast the pork for 10 more minutes. Remove the pork from the oven and allow to rest in a warm place for 10 minutes.

Meanwhile, fry the pak choi in a little groundnut oil. Once softened, add 100ml water, the lemon juice and soy sauce to the pan.

Cut the meat into slices about 1cm thick and serve with the fried pak choi and sprinkled with spring onion. Serve with noodles.

Homemade sausages

SERVES 8

2kg lean pork, such as shoulder

1 tablespoon Maldon sea salt

1 tablespoon cracked black
  peppercorns

bunch of fresh curly parsley, chopped

8 fresh plums, peeled, stoned and
  puréed

bunch of fresh sage, chopped

½ tablespoon fresh lemon thyme,
  chopped

½ tablespoon fresh oregano, chopped

½ tablespoon grated nutmeg

200g fresh breadcrumbs

150ml red wine

approx. 90cm hog casings, rinsed
  with cold water and left to soak in
  clean water

Dice the pork and pass it through a meat grinder using a fine cutting blade. Season with salt and pepper. Add the parsley, plums, sage, lemon thyme, oregano and nutmeg. Using your hands, mix well into the mince. Add the breadcrumbs and wine and mix well. Place into an airtight container and refrigerate for 1 hour.

Once your mince is rested, put through the meat grinder one last time using a fine cutting blade.

Pass the hog skin over the sausage nozzle on a sausage machine, pinch the loose end of the hog casing together and pass the mince through the machine until the mix has run out.

When making the sausages by hand, fill a large piping bag with the mince. Pass the hog skin over the nozzle, holding it in place with your fingers. Tie a knot in the hog skin, and leave the first bit of skin empty. Push the mince into the skin, trying to fill the skin as evenly as you can. Release the skin over the nozzle as you go. (See pictures page 96.)

Pinch and twist your sausages at 10–15cm lengths and refrigerate for 1 hour before cooking.

Spiced lamb with cheese and spinach potatoes

SERVES 3–4

1 shoulder of lamb, boned and cut
  into three pieces
1kg King Edward potatoes, cut into
  large wedges
1 tablespoon cayenne pepper
pinch of salt
1 tablespoon white semolina flour
1 tablespoon garlic salt
60ml olive oil
500g spinach
400g goat's cheese

FOR THE MARINADE

3 garlic cloves, crushed
1 fresh red chilli, deseeded and
  chopped
1 tablespoon tomato purée
10 anchovy fillets, finely chopped
1 tablespoon paprika
zest and juice of 1 lemon
10 sprigs of fresh thyme, leaves
  picked and chopped
1 teaspoon sugar
60ml olive oil

FOR THE DRESSING

1 large shallot, finely chopped
bunch of fresh mint, finely chopped
1 tablespoon red wine vinegar
1 tablespoon Dijon mustard

Mix all the marinade ingredients together in a bowl. Add the lamb, mix to cover the lamb in the marinade and leave in the fridge to marinate for a minimum of 2 hours (ideally overnight).

Preheat the oven to 180°C/350°F/gas mark 4.

Remove the lamb from the marinade and set the marinade aside. Heat a frying pan and seal the lamb until brown on all sides. Place on a baking tray and cook in the oven for 55 minutes.

Meanwhile, blanch the potatoes in boiling salted water for 7 minutes. Drain and allow to cool. In a bowl, combine the cayenne pepper, salt, semolina flour and garlic salt. Toss the potatoes in the dry marinade to coat them evenly. Drizzle with the oil.

Turn the oven temperature down to 160°C/325°F/gas mark 3. Pour the reserved marinade over the lamb and cook in the oven for a further 40 minutes. At the same time, roast the potatoes.

Pan-fry the spinach until wilted. Drain and roughly chop. Flake the goat's cheese into a bowl and then mix through the spinach. Add the roasted potatoes and toss together.

Mix all the dressing ingredients together in a bowl and serve with the lamb and potatoes.

Herb and mustard-crusted best end of lamb

SERVES 4

2 carrots, chopped

150g new potatoes, chopped

50g baby turnips, chopped

50g Puy lentils

50g butter, plus an extra knob

1 tablespoon sugar

olive oil

whole best end of lamb, trimmed of
fat and cut in half

5 sprigs of fresh rosemary

50g breadcrumbs

salt and freshly ground black pepper

2 tablespoons Dijon mustard

a bunch of fresh mint, chopped

3 tablespoons red wine vinegar

FOR THE GRAVY

50g butter, plus an extra knob

1 onion, finely chopped

1 garlic clove, finely chopped

trimmings from the vegetables

1 glass of red wine

500ml lamb or vegetable stock (see
page 231)

Preheat the oven to 180°C/350°F/gas mark 4.

Put the vegetables and lentils into a pan. Cover with water, add 50g butter and the sugar and boil hard until all the water has evaporated.

Meanwhile, heat 2 tablespoons olive oil in a pan over a high heat and sear the two pieces of lamb to seal in the juices. Strip the leaves off the rosemary (set aside the stalks), and mix the rosemary with the breadcrumbs and season. Brush the seared lamb with the mustard, then roll it in the breadcrumb mixture to create a crust. Place on a roasting tray and roast in the oven for 25 minutes.

To make the gravy, melt the butter in a frying pan and gently soften the onion, garlic and any vegetable trimmings.

When the lamb is cooked, remove from the tray, cover with tinfoil and allow to rest.

Pour the fat out of the roasting tray. Scoop the onion mixture into the tray and place on a low heat. Add the red wine and rosemary stalks and scrape any lamb sediments into the juices. Pour this mixture back into a saucepan, add the stock and reduce by three quarters over a high heat.

Finish the vegetables with the mint, a knob of butter and the red wine vinegar. Add a knob of butter to the gravy, sieve and serve over the lamb and vegetables.

Lamb fillets with olives, capers and tomato

This is great with a baked potato and fresh vegetables.

SERVES 4

4 teaspoons olive oil

1kg lamb neck fillets, cut into 2.5cm
  chunks

20 spiced, peppered salami slices

3 tablespoons red wine vinegar

1 teaspoon sugar

2 tablespoons capers

100ml chicken or vegetable stock
  (see pages 230-1)

150g pitted black olives

2 sprigs of fresh rosemary

1 x 400g tin chopped tomatoes

FOR THE YOGHURT DRESSING

a bunch of fresh mint, finely chopped

3 garlic cloves, finely chopped

½ cucumber, peeled, deseeded and
  finely chopped

250ml yoghurt

salt and freshly ground black pepper

Heat the olive oil in a large casserole pot until smoking. Add the lamb fillet chunks and cook over a high heat until browned. Add the salami and cook for 1 minute, then pour in the vinegar and sugar and stir until caramelised. Stir in the capers and stock. Add the olives, rosemary and tomatoes, turn the heat to low, cover with tinfoil and cook gently for 1 hour and 20 minutes.

For the yoghurt dressing, mix together the mint, garlic, cucumber and yoghurt with a pinch of salt and pepper.

Serve the lamb with the yoghurt dressing on top.

Welsh lamb, mint and whisky burgers

The combination of lamb and seaweed is not only very Welsh but also memorable...

MAKES 4

800g Welsh lamb, minced

2 tablespoons chopped fresh mint

2 teaspoons whisky

1 egg, beaten

100g laver bread (see Ed's tip page
  25)

450g Caerphilly cheese, grated

1 leek, thoroughly rinsed and chopped

100g smoked bacon, diced

4 burger buns, sliced in half

Mix together the minced lamb, mint, whisky, egg and laver bread, and mould into four burgers.

Fry the burgers in a medium hot frying pan for 4 to 5 minutes on each side.

Place the cheese in a bowl. Fry the leek and bacon in the burger fat for 1 to 2 minutes, then add to the grated cheese.

Serve the burgers in the buns, topped with the leek, bacon and cheese mixture.

Chicken thighs stuffed with Stilton and walnuts

This dish is very similar to chicken Cordon Bleu, although I've altered it somewhat to make it easier to prepare and to give a slightly stronger, more adult feel.

SERVES 4

50g walnuts, roughly chopped
50g dried breadcrumbs
200g Stilton cheese, crumbled
50g butter
1 onion, finely chopped
bunch of fresh sage, leaves chopped,
  or 1 teaspoon dried sage
1 tablespoon port
50ml double cream
salt and freshly ground black pepper
4 x 200g chicken thighs, skin on but
  boned (ask your butcher)
vegetable oil
500g runner beans, finely sliced
25g butter
1 tablespoon wholegrain mustard

FOR THE FENNEL MASH

1 fennel bulb, cut into 4 wedges
knob of butter
1 teaspoon ground fennel seeds
450g mashed potatoes

Preheat the oven to 180°C/350°F/gas mark 4.

Toast the walnuts under the grill or in a pan with a little vegetable oil until brown. Don't burn them! In a large bowl, mix together the breadcrumbs, toasted walnuts and Stilton. Set aside.

To make the stuffing, melt the butter in a frying pan and gently fry the onions. Add the sage and port and pour into the breadcrumb mixture while it's still warm. Add the cream and some seasoning and carefully mix together.

Open up the chicken thighs and divide the stuffing equally between them. Using butcher's string, tie the thighs up into little parcels, put on to a plate and refrigerate for 30 minutes to firm up.

Boil the fennel for 40 minutes in salted water until very, very soft.

Meanwhile, heat a tablespoon of vegetable oil and place in an ovenproof pan on a moderate heat until the oil is hot but not smoking. Add the chicken thighs, sliced side up, and gently move the pan around to ensure they don't stick. Place into the oven and cook for 35 to 40 minutes.

After the chicken has had about 30 minutes in the oven, boil the runner beans in salted water for 10 minutes. Drain and toss in the butter and mustard. Season with some salt and pepper.

Drain the fennel and melt a little butter in the pot you boiled the fennel in. Add the fennel and ground fennel seeds, stir briefly, then place into a food processor and blitz until smooth. Fold into the mashed potatoes.

Serve the chicken with the fennel mash and mustard beans.

White cooked chicken

In this book we're celebrating modern British cookery, and this includes ingredients and cooking methods from all over the globe, from just about every port that merchants landed at. That's why you'll find there are a few sensational ethnic recipes on these pages. One of these is this Cantonese-style chicken, which I think is far superior to the traditional bung-it-in-and-walk-away method us Brits favour. You can use the stock left over as a base for Asian-style soups, or reduce it down to make a rich gravy.

SERVES 4

75ml dry sherry

5 large shallots, trimmed

12 garlic cloves

thumb-sized piece of fresh ginger, roughly chopped

sea salt

1.6kg free range chicken

1 litre vegetable oil

freshly ground Szechuan pepper

FOR THE DRESSING

3 shallots, finely sliced

2cm piece of fresh ginger, finely sliced

small bunch of fresh coriander, finely chopped

3 tablespoons ketjap manis (see page 87)

3 tablespoons light soy sauce

3 tablespoons Chinese or malt vinegar

1 fresh red chilli, finely chopped

3 tablespoons vegetable oil

Put 6 litres of water into a large saucepan and add the sherry, shallots, garlic cloves, chopped ginger and 2 tablespoons sea salt. Bring to the boil and simmer for 15 minutes. Rinse the chicken under cold water and lower, breast side down, into the stock. Poach gently for 15 minutes – do not allow the liquid to boil. Remove from the heat and allow the chicken to sit in the cooling stock for 3 hours.

Gently lift the chicken from the stock, pouring all the liquid out of the cavity. Place on a tray and allow to cool completely. Using a large pair of scissors, cut the chicken in half along the breastbone and, with a bread knife, saw through the backbone. Refrigerate the chicken halves for at least 2 hours to dry the skin; the drier the skin, the crispier it will become.

At this point you can either roast or fry the chicken. Roast it by brushing it with a little oil and salt and placing in a hot oven for 30 minutes to crisp up.

To fry the chicken, cut each half into drumstick, thigh and breast. Heat the oil in a deep, steady pan (ideally in a wok) to about 160°C/325°F or until a whole garlic clove dropped in the oil starts to fizz. Lower the chicken pieces, meatiest sides down, into the oil and fry for 5 minutes or until the skin is golden brown. Using tongs, carefully lift the chicken from the oil; try not to tear the skin. Drain on kitchen paper and allow to rest.

Combine all the dressing ingredients in a bowl.

Using a large knife, cut the chicken into chunks and arrange on a plate. Finish with a drizzle of the dressing, shallot slices, a pinch of salt and Szechuan pepper. Serve immediately with either rice or noodles.

Plum and blue Wensleydale chicken

SERVES 2

2 skinless, boneless chicken breasts

salt and freshly ground black pepper

1 small ripe plum, halved, stoned and
thinly sliced

75g blue Wensleydale cheese, thinly
sliced

4 slices of Parma ham

1 tablespoon olive oil

knob of butter

150ml dry white wine

2 tablespoons crème fraîche

Using a sharp knife, carefully cut horizontally down the side of each chicken breast so they are almost cut in half. Open out flat like a book and place between two sheets of clingfilm. Lay on a firm board and bash each one with a rolling pin to flatten.

Season the chicken breasts on both sides and arrange slices of plum and cheese over one half of each breast. Fold over the other half to enclose the filling, then wrap each breast in two slices of Parma ham, pressing them securely to the chicken.

Heat the oil and butter in a shallow pan with a lid. When the mixture is hot and foaming, add the chicken and fry on both sides for about 5 minutes until the ham is crisp.

Pour in the wine and bring to the boil. Reduce the heat and cover. Cook gently for 20 to 25 minutes, turning halfway through cooking, until the chicken is tender and thoroughly cooked and the juices run clear when the breast is pierced with a fork.

Stir the crème fraîche into the pan, scraping up any sediment from the base of the pan. Taste and add more seasoning if necessary. Serve the chicken on warmed plates, with the sauce poured around.

Chicken thighs stuffed with haggis

This recipe was first introduced to me by a French chef who worked for me a number of years ago; I then took it with me to serve as part of a banquet in Chengdu, Szechuan province, China. Usually when you explain the content of haggis to an audience, they struggle somewhat, but in Chengdu they were absolutely delighted. As they put it, 'all the good bit go in'. In a competition to name this dish in a Chinese way, the winner described it as 'three shades of silk over the Hoo Fun Lake'.

SERVES 4

4 boneless chicken thighs

225g haggis

1 tablespoon vegetable oil

1 onion, finely chopped

2 garlic cloves, finely chopped

75g butter

400g fresh spinach, washed and torn

salt and freshly ground black pepper

good pinch of nutmeg

450g mashed potatoes, to serve

FOR THE WHISKY SAUCE

200ml whisky

1 bay leaf

400ml chicken stock (see page 230)

1 teaspoon butter

Preheat the oven to 180°C/350°F/gas mark 4.

Open the chicken thighs and divide the haggis filling evenly between them. Form the chicken into parcels and tie with string. Place the parcels in the fridge for 30 minutes to firm a little.

Put the oil in a large ovenproof frying pan and place over a moderate heat. Add the chicken thighs skin side down and cook for 2 minutes. Place in the oven for 35 to 40 minutes.

While the chicken is cooking, gently fry the onion and garlic in butter, add the spinach, cook until any water has evaporated and season with salt,

pepper and nutmeg. Set aside.

Remove the chicken from the oven and turn off the heat. Place the chicken in a clean ovenproof dish and put back in the oven to keep warm.

To make the sauce, pour the fat from the frying pan, add the whisky to the pan and place back on the heat over a low flame. Reduce the whisky down by two thirds, add the bay leaf and stock. Bring to

the boil, reduce by two thirds, season and stir in the butter. and remove from the heat.

Serve the haggis-stuffed chicken with the spinach, mashed potatoes and whisky sauce. Enjoy!

ED'S TIP: Do not look into the pan once you've added the whisky as it might ignite. If it does, don't panic; it will die down by itself.

Crispy-skinned pheasant with Szechuan pepper

SERVES 2–4

2 pheasants

1 litre vegetable oil

½ teaspoon ground Szechuan pepper

1 teaspoon Maldon sea salt

1 spring onion, chopped

juice of ½ lemon

FOR THE STOCK

2.5 litres chicken stock (see page 230)

250ml dry sherry

300ml dark soy sauce

200g demerara sugar

1 whole garlic bulb, cloves crushed

4cm piece of fresh ginger, roughly chopped

5 shallots, cut in half and trimmed

10 star anise

4 cinnamon sticks

1 teaspoon Chinese five-spice powder

zest of 1 orange

Place all the stock ingredients in a large saucepan, bring to the boil and simmer for 20 minutes.

Thoroughly wash the pheasants, then lower them into the stock, breast side down, and allow them to poach gently for 10 minutes. Remove from the heat and allow them to steep in the stock for 3 hours at room temperature.

Using tongs, remove the pheasants and place them, breast up, on a wire rack over a tray to drain and cool. Dry the skin of the pheasants with a hairdryer until the texture resembles greaseproof paper – the drier the skin, the crispier.

In a deep-sided pan, heat the oil. Lower the pheasants into the oil breast side down and fry for 4 minutes; the pheasants will take on a dark appearance. Using tongs, remove, drain on kitchen paper and allow to rest for 10 minutes. With a bread knife, saw the birds in half and then, with a large chopping knife, slice the meat off the bone and cut the breast into pieces. Remove the legs and slice in the same way.

Serve with a sprinkle of Szechuan pepper, Maldon salt and chopped spring onion, and the lemon juice squeezed over.

Pheasant in red wine with mash

SERVES 2

4 Maris Piper potatoes, peeled and
   chopped
1 small swede, chopped
3 parsnips, peeled
150g unsalted butter
3 rashers of streaky bacon
5 shallots, sliced
6 small mushrooms, sliced
2 pheasant breasts
1 tablespoon plain flour
300ml chicken stock
1 teaspoon tomato purée
1 tablespoon redcurrant jelly
sprig of fresh marjoram, cut up with
   scissors
sprig of fresh thyme, cut up with
   scissors
150ml red wine
salt and freshly ground black pepper
1 tablespoon honey

Preheat the oven to 180°C/350°F/gas mark 4.

Place the potatoes and swede into a pot of boiling water and cook for 20 minutes. Place the parsnips in a separate pan of boiling water and boil for 6 minutes.

Heat 50g butter in a frying pan and fry the bacon with the shallots over a moderate heat for 2 minutes or until the shallots turn brown. Add the mushrooms and cook for a further 5 minutes. Transfer the contents of the frying pan into a casserole dish but retain the cooking fats for browning the pheasant.

Return the frying pan to a moderate heat and brown the pheasant breasts for 2 minutes before adding to the casserole dish. Add the flour to the empty, but juicy, frying pan and cook for 2 minutes before adding the stock, tomato purée, redcurrant jelly, herbs and finally the red wine. Bring to the boil and then pour over the pheasant breasts. Then place the casserole dish in the oven to cook for 20 minutes.

Drain the parsnips and pour over the honey. Place the honey-coated parsnips in a roasting tray and cook in the oven for 20 minutes.

Strain the swede and potatoes and mash together with 100g butter and season well. Pile on a serving dish and put the parsnips on top. Slice the pheasant breasts and arrange on top of the mash. Scoop out the mushrooms and onions from the casserole juice and then swirl the sauce over the top.

Slow-cooked pheasant casserole

SERVES 4

2 pheasants
3 tablespoons sunflower oil
225g smoked bacon scraps, diced
3 large onions, chopped
4 celery sticks, roughly chopped
3 carrots, chopped
225g swede, chopped
1 large red pepper, chopped
100g wild mushrooms, chopped
1 whole garlic bulb, cloves crushed
100g chorizo, cut into thick chunks
1 tablespoon plain flour
300ml chicken stock (see page 230)
300ml red wine
1 tablespoon redcurrant jelly
1 tablespoon Worcestershire sauce
salt and freshly ground black pepper
1 tablespoon chopped fresh herbs
   (parsley and thyme are ideal)
lightly steamed green beans, to serve

FOR THE CHAMP POTATOES
1kg floury potatoes, quartered
250ml whole milk
50g butter
bunch of spring onions, chopped

Preheat the oven to 120°C/250°F/gas mark ½.

Tie the legs of each bird tightly together. Heat the oil in a casserole dish on the hob and add the pheasants. Brown them all over in the oil, then remove from the dish and set aside on a plate.

In the same casserole dish, fry the bacon, then add all the chopped vegetables, mushrooms, garlic and chorizo and stir in the flour thoroughly. Add the stock, wine, jelly and Worcestershire sauce and bring to the boil. Add the pheasants, put on the lid and transfer to the oven, cooking very slowly for 3 to 4 hours until the meat is tender.

In a saucepan, cook the potatoes in boiling water for 20 minutes. In a separate pan, heat the milk and butter and bring to the boil. Add the spring onions to the milk, then remove from the heat and leave to infuse for about 1 minute. Mash the potatoes and stir in the milk mixture until everything is smooth. Check for seasoning and add salt if necessary.

Lift the birds out of the pot, place on a plate and leave until cool enough to handle. Pull all the meat off the bones and return to the casserole dish. Season to taste and add the fresh herbs.

Serve in a big fat soup plate with steamed green beans, champ potatoes and the cooking sauce ladled over.

Guinea fowl with roast red onions

SERVES 2

1 guinea fowl, cut into breasts (bone on), thighs and drumsticks
60g butter
pinch of fresh nutmeg
salt and freshly ground black pepper
6 rashers of smoked streaky bacon
2 large red onions, quartered (keep the root on)
2 tablespoons olive oil
2 teaspoons balsamic vinegar
1 teaspoon cayenne pepper
2 Maris Piper potatoes, quartered
250ml chicken stock (see page 230)

FOR THE MEDLAR SAUCE
250ml red wine
400ml chicken stock (see page 230)
1 tablespoon medlar jelly

Preheat the oven to 180°C/350°F/gas mark 4.

Rub the guinea fowl with half the butter, sprinkle with nutmeg and season. Wrap each piece in a rasher of bacon and place in a roasting tray.

Drizzle the onions with olive oil and balsamic vinegar, season and place alongside the guinea fowl.

In a separate dish, melt the remaining butter with the cayenne pepper. Toss the potatoes in the butter, then pour in the chicken stock.

Roast the guinea fowl and potatoes in the oven for 40 minutes. Remove the guinea fowl and onions from the roasting tray and set aside.

To make the sauce, transfer the roasting tray to the hob and deglaze with the red wine and chicken stock, reducing by one fifth. Stir in the medlar jelly, strain and pour over the guinea, red onions and fondant potatoes.

Partridge with braised beetroot and swede purée

This is an Chinese-inspired way of cooking game. The steaming moistens and tenderises the meat and takes away any bitter flavours.

SERVES 2

1 whole partridge
1 tablespoon green peppercorns in
  brine
2 shallots, finely chopped
50g butter
1 garlic clove
4 preboiled beetroot
6 rashers of crispy bacon
6 chunks white crusty bread
vegetable oil or lard
1 teaspoon Chinese five-spice powder
½ teaspoon salt

FOR THE SWEDE PURÉE

1 small swede, peeled and cut into
  2.5cm cubes
50g butter
1 shallot, finely chopped
50ml single cream
salt and freshly ground black pepper
good pinch fresh nutmeg

FOR THE SALAD

1 tablespoon truffle oil
1 teaspoon olive oil
juice of ½ lemon
4 celery sticks, finely sliced
bunch of watercress

FOR THE STEAMING WATER

2 garlic cloves, unpeeled
vegetable peelings (any will do)
1 teaspoon sugar
2 tablespoons sherry
1 tablespoon soy sauce
squeeze of lemon juice

Preheat the oven to 220°C/425°F/gas mark 7.

To make the swede purée, boil the swede in a pan of water for at least 40 minutes so that it is completely soft and all the fibres in the vegetable have broken down. Gently melt the butter in a pan and soften the shallots over a low heat. Add the swede and cook for 4 to 5 minutes over a moderate heat to remove all the moisture.

When the swede has become dry with a slightly translucent appearance, move the pan off the heat and start to mash. Add the cream, salt, pepper and nutmeg.

Add all the ingredients for the steaming to the bottom of a steamer with 300ml water and steam the partridge for 20 minutes. Remove and pat dry. Allow the bird to dry properly.

Vigorously reduce the steaming liquor. When it becomes slightly syrupy, strain it off, add the green peppercorns and hold on a gentle simmer.

Gently soften the shallots in a large pan with half the butter. Add the garlic and then the beetroot and cook gently for 5 minutes. Add a tablespoon of the green peppercorn sauce and allow to caramelise.

Wrap the bacon around the chunks of bread and thread on to two wooden skewers.

Heat 1 tablespoon vegetable oil or lard in a large ovenproof pan and seal the partridge on all sides. Sprinkle the Chinese 5 spice powder and salt inside the bird. Place the bacon and bread skewers by the side of the partridge and cook in the preheated oven for 10 minutes.

Mix the truffle and olive oils with the lemon juice and dress the celery and watercress.

To serve, use a bread knife to saw the partridge in half and cut into pieces. Arrange over the braised beetroots and truffle and watercress salad with the swede purée on the side. Finish by pouring more green peppercorn sauce over the bird.

Roast grouse with bacon-wrapped chicory

I have to dedicate this recipe to an old school friend of mine who, before he found his fame and fortune, was very concerned about me losing my way as a professional chef. He went to a specialist deli and bought two grey grouse, a black truffle, a bottle of wine and some good-quality veal stock. He called me up, invited me over and thrust the ingredients at me. Forty minutes later we sat down and had one of my most memorable meals. This friend of mine likes to keep things discrete, but I'd like to say a big thank you over the years for the moments of kindness that have meant so much.

SERVES 2

2 grouse
salt and freshly ground black pepper
4 good sprigs of thyme
50g pork fat or beef dripping
2 large floury potatoes
50ml whole milk
100g butter
1 small black truffle (available from a
   good deli), grated
400ml dry red wine
400ml beef stock (see page 230) or
   veal stock
apple jelly (or homemade crab apple
   and lavender jelly, page 234), to
   serve

FOR THE BACON-WRAPPED CHICORY

50g butter
4 heads of chicory, cut in half
   lengthways
1 small onion, finely chopped
2 garlic cloves, finely chopped
bunch of fresh curly parsley, chopped
400ml vegetable stock (see page
   231)
8 rashers of streaky bacon

Preheat the oven to 180°C/350°F/gas mark 4.

Take the grouse, sprinkle with salt and pepper and push 2 sprigs of thyme into the cavity of each bird. Heat the dripping in a large, ovenproof frying pan until it smokes and seal the birds on all sides until they're biscuit-brown. Remove the pan from the heat and place the birds on a chopping board.

Melt the butter for the chicory in the pan you sealed the birds in, off the heat. Add the chicory and cook gently over a moderate heat to colour lightly on all sides. Remove from the pan and place on a chopping board to cool.

Add the onion and garlic to the pan and soften. Add the parsley and stock. Remove from the heat.

Wrap each chicory half in a bacon spiral, being careful not to overlap the bacon, and place flat side down into the stock. Cover the pan with foil and cook in the oven. After 30 minutes, remove the foil and cook for a further 10 to 15 minutes until all the stock has evaporated.

Transfer the chicory on to a heatproof plate and scrape out the onions, garlic and any residual juice over the top. Cover with a piece of foil and set aside.

Turn the oven up to 220°C/425°F/gas mark 7.

Place the grouse into the scraped frying pan and cook in the oven for 20 to 25 minutes.

Cook the potatoes in boiling water for 20 minutes. Drain and mash well with the milk and half the butter. Season to taste and set aside.

Stir the remaining butter with the truffle and a pinch of salt into a paste and place to one side.

Add the red wine to a saucepan and boil until it has reduced by half, then add the stock and reduce down to one fifth. Finish by adding the truffle butter and seasoning.

Remove the grouse from the oven, cover with foil and allow to rest for 5 minutes.

Reheat your mash and add a dollop to each plate. Place the chicory on the side and the grouse next to it. Pour over the hot truffle gravy and top with a spoonful of apple jelly.

Venison with honey roast vegetables

I can't remember who it was, but I saw some fellow on the box cooking rib of venison. I immediately called my butcher, placed an order, spent the following morning in the kitchen and put this recipe together. It's got a very autumn/winter feel to it. The cut of venison I'm using is similar to, but smaller than, the French cut known as *côte de boeuf* or, as we know it in England, rib eye on the bone.

SERVES 2

pinch of salt

4 medium carrots, cut into large chunks

2 parsnips, cut into large chunks

2 large turnips, cut into large chunks

1 small celeriac, cut into large chunks

1 whole smoked garlic bulb, cloves separated

8 small shallots, peeled

2 tablespoons honey

1 tablespoon wholegrain mustard

4 tablespoons vegetable oil

small bunch of fresh curly parsley, chopped

25g lard

2 x 250g venison steaks, cut on the rib

salt and freshly ground black pepper

1 glass of red wine

1 bay leaf

600ml beef stock (see page 230)

Preheat the oven to 180°C/350°F/gas mark 4. Line a large oven tray with greaseproof paper.

Take a large saucepan and fill it with water. Add a good pinch of salt and bring to the boil. In batches, blanch the vegetables in the boiling water for 4 minutes, scooping them out into a colander when done. Lastly, blanch the smoked garlic cloves and shallots. Tip all the vegetables on to a large tea towel and dry them as thoroughly as you can, then transfer them to the oven tray.

Blend together the honey and mustard and whisk in the vegetable oil. Mix the root vegetables together with the chopped parsley and mustard and honey dressing, place in the middle of the oven and cook for 15 minutes.

Heat the lard in a large frying pan over a high heat and seal the venison ribs on both sides. Season with salt and pepper.

Place the venison steaks on a rack in the oven over the vegetables and cook for a further 20 to 25 minutes. Remove the venison from the oven and place back into the frying pan, off the heat. Cover with foil and allow the meat to rest while continuing to cook the vegetables for a further 5 minutes.

Put the wine and the bay leaf in a saucepan and bring to the boil. Reduce by half, add the beef stock and gently reduce again, by three quarters.

To serve, slice the venison and serve on individual plates with a pile of the honey roast vegetables and the gravy drizzled over.

Venison Nelson

This is similar to a beef Wellington, but it uses venison as an alternative to beef and was apparently favoured by Lord Nelson.

SERVES 2
1 teaspoon crushed juniper berries
1 teaspoon crushed black
  peppercorns
250ml tawny port
1 bay leaf
good pinch of salt
½ teaspoon mixed dry herbs
500g loin venison, trimmed of fat
1 tablespoon vegetable oil
250g puff pastry (see page 226)
1 egg, beaten

FOR THE CHICKEN LIVER PÂTÉ
1 onion, finely chopped
1 garlic clove, crushed
125g butter
50g mixed wild mushrooms, sliced
1 teaspoon vegetable oil
300g free-range chicken livers, cut
  into pieces
150ml port
salt and freshly ground black pepper

Put the juniper berries, peppercorns, port, bay leaf, salt and herbs in a small bowl, add the venison, cover and marinate for at least 1 hour in the fridge.

Preheat to oven to 180°C/350°F/gas mark 4.

For the pâté, gently sweat the onion and garlic in half the butter for 10 minutes. Increase the heat, add the sliced mushrooms and cook until coloured and softened. Remove from the pan, place on a plate and set aside.

Place the clean pan back on the hob and heat the vegetable oil over a high heat. Add the chicken livers and fry until brown on all sides. Remove from the heat, put the mushrooms and onion mixture back into the pan, and add the port and seasoning.

Gently simmer for 4 minutes, allow to cool, then blend in a food processor until smooth, gradually adding the remaining butter. Set aside in a cool area, but not in the fridge.

Remove the venison from the marinade and dab dry with kitchen paper.

In a wide pan, heat 1 tablespoon vegetable oil until hot and flash-fry the venison for a few seconds. Turn the heat down and cook for a further 5 minutes, then set aside to cool.

Roll the pastry out into an A4-sized rectangle, about 5mm thick, and generously spread the middle with most of the chicken liver pâté, leaving a margin of about 2cm around the edge. Place the venison in the centre of the pastry and spread the remaining pâté on top of the meat. Brush the edges of the pastry with the beaten egg and then roll the pastry around the meat, sealing the sides as you go and decorating with any leftover pastry. Cook in the oven for 20 minutes, then remove and leave to rest for 10 minutes.

To serve, cut into four thick slices. Ideally, finish with a drizzle of Cumberland sauce (see page 233) and vegetables of your choice.

Slow-roasted rabbit

Rabbit is one of the most sustainable wild foods we have in Britain. With fewer and fewer predators in the wild, there are rabbits in abundance. People seem to feel strange eating these cute creatures, but once you've skinned a rabbit, it appears just as edible as any other meat in the butcher's shop.

Here, I have added dried wild mushrooms; the type usually described as ceps or, if imported from Italy, *porcini*. Traditionally known as penny bun mushrooms, they grow in abundance throughout woodlands in the autumn. In Italy, they will fight to the death to find a good patch of these but, fortunately for me, there seem to be very few mushroom pickers in England and, on a good day, I've collected kilos of them.

SERVES 6–8

2 whole rabbits

50g dried ceps (penny buns)

1.2 litres vegetable or chicken stock
(see pages 230–1) or rabbit stock

1 tablespoon vegetable oil

175g butter

4 small onions, finely chopped

1 leek, finely chopped

100g chestnut mushrooms, quartered

1 tablespoon flour

salt and freshly ground black pepper

bunch of fresh curly parsley, chopped

400ml dry white wine

½ teaspoon salt

½ teaspoon white pepper

2 bay leaves

100g barley

2 tablespoons wholegrain mustard

175g smoked streaky bacon, sliced

100ml double cream

lightly steamed green vegetables, to
serve

FOR THE GARLIC MASH

1 whole garlic bulb, cloves separated

6 large potatoes, peeled and cut into
large chunks

150ml milk

75g butter

bunch of fresh curly parsley, chopped

Joint the rabbits by cutting them each into six, two joints from the front, two from the middle and two from the rear. If you're not sure, ask your butcher to do it for you.

Soak the dried mushrooms in 600ml boiling water until the water has cooled. Remove the mushrooms and squeeze them dry over the soaking water. Place the stock in a saucepan and strain the mushroom liquid through kitchen paper into the stock to remove any grit. Bring to a very gentle rolling boil.

In a large casserole dish or deep-sided roasting dish, heat the oil and melt half the butter. Seal the rabbit pieces on all sides until golden brown and remove from the casserole dish. Set aside on a plate.

Now add the rest of the butter, onions and leek and soften for 3 minutes over a moderate heat. Add the squeezed mushrooms and cook for a further minute, then add the chestnut mushrooms, stir and cook for a couple more minutes. Sprinkle in the flour, season with salt and pepper and stir thoroughly. Add the parsley, pour in the wine and bring to the boil. Pour in the stock, add the bay leaves, barley and mustard. Then lay in the pieces of rabbit, cover and cook on the lowest heat for 1 hour 20 minutes.

While the casserole is cooking, preheat the oven to 180°C/350°F/gas mark 4. Cover a roasting tray with parchment paper and place the strips of bacon on top.

For the garlic mash, blanch the unpeeled garlic cloves in boiling water for 5 minutes, then remove and place around the bacon on the roasting tray. Roast for 20 to 25 minutes until the bacon is nice and crisp. Meanwhile, cook the potatoes in boiling water for 20 minutes. Then drain and mash well with the butter and milk.

Peel the roasted garlic, mash the flesh into a purée and fold into the potato with the chopped parsley.

Remove the lid from the casserole dish and allow to cook gently on the hob for a further 15 minutes, skimming off any fat on the surface.

Finish by stirring in the cream and scattering over the crispy bacon. Season to taste and serve with the garlic mash and steamed green vegetables.

ED'S TIP: To dry your own mushrooms, slice thinly, lay on greaseproof paper and pop into the airing cupboard for a couple of weeks.

Duck confit with braised fennel and red cabbage

You can prepare the duck in advance and keep it refrigerated, or you can buy duck confit in a jar from a quality retailer. If bought in a jar, remove the duck from the fat and ignore the first paragraph of the recipe instructions.

SERVES 4

4 duck legs

5 fresh bay leaves

sprigs of fresh thyme

1 tablespoon salt

½ teaspoon black peppercorns

1 litre vegetable oil

4 large potatoes, peeled and cut into chunks

50g butter

200ml whole milk

1 tablespoon wholegrain mustard

FOR THE FENNEL AND RED CABBAGE

1 fennel bulb, finely sliced

½ small red cabbage, very finely sliced

1 teaspoon ground star anise

½ teaspoon finely ground cloves

1 bay leaf

½ teaspoon salt

pinch of freshly ground black pepper

4 teaspoons muscovado sugar

300ml orange juice

100ml raisins

100ml red wine vinegar

FOR THE PEAR JUS

1 pear, peeled, cored and cut into 12 segments

1 tablespoon Poire William or brandy

200ml veal or beef stock

25g butter

salt and freshly ground black pepper

Put the duck legs, bay leaves, thyme, salt and peppercorns in a large bowl. Mix well and set aside for 30 minutes. Pour the oil into a deep-sided pot, add the duck and marinade ingredients and cook gently on the lowest heat on the hob for 3 hours. Remove from the heat and allow the oil to cool.

Preheat the oven to 150°C/300°/gas mark 2.

Place all the ingredients for the fennel and red cabbage in a roasting tray, cover with foil and bake for 90 minutes, stirring every 30 minutes.

Take a large frying pan with a heatproof handle, place the duck legs, skin side down, into the frying pan and bring up to the heat on the hob. Fry over a moderate heat for 2 minutes, then remove from the heat and turn the duck legs over. Add 100ml water to the pan, cover with foil and cook in the oven for 20 minutes.

Cook the potatoes in boiling water for 20 minutes. Drain and mash well with the butter, milk and wholegrain mustard.

For the pear jus, gently poach the pear segments with the Poire William or brandy. Pour the stock over the pears and alcohol and reduce by three quarters. Finish by adding the butter and seasoning.

Serve the duck with the braised fennel and red cabbage, with the mash on the side and accompanied by the jus.

ED'S TIP: The duck should be cooked very, very slowly and gently to ensure it does not toughen but becomes extremely tender.

Jellied chicken and ham pie

You might not be familiar with hot water pastry, but it's the same pastry used for pork pies. It's not commonly made at home any more, and I don't know why as it's so simple to make and really very good.

Ham hocks are about the cheapest meat you can buy from the butcher and they go a long way. Mixing this with some cooked chicken and baking it makes for a delicious cold meal. For me this is a fantastic summer lunchtime recipe. It goes beautifully with a spoonful of English mustard, a crisp green salad, a side of pickled onions and half a pint of mild.

SERVES 4

1 x 350g ham hock
1 teaspoon white wine vinegar
450g chicken thighs and legs
1 large leek, thoroughly rinsed and
  chopped
1 onion, chopped
2 large carrots, chopped
bunch of fresh curly parsley, chopped
½ teaspoon mace
¼ teaspoon white pepper
½ teaspoon mustard powder
¼ teaspoon celery salt
500g hot water pastry (see page
  226)
flour, for dusting
beef dripping or vegetable oil
salt

Place the ham hock in a large pan. Add the vinegar and 2 litres water and cook for 3 hours. Remove the ham, allow to cool and place the chicken into the pan. Poach the chicken for 30 minutes in the ham stock, then lift out of the pan and allow to cool. Strip the ham and chicken meat from the bone and place into a large bowl.

Put the leek, onion and carrots into the stock, bring to the boil and allow to cook for 10 minutes.

Drain the vegetables, reserving the stock, and place in the bowl with the meat. Add the chopped parsley, mace, pepper, mustard powder and celery salt and mix everything together.

Place the stock back on the hob and reduce down to a concentrated stock of about 300ml. Allow to cool. Stir 6 tablespoons of this reduced stock into the vegetable and meat mixture.

Roll out the pastry on a floured surface. Grease a pie plate (see tip) liberally with beef dripping or vegetable oil. Sprinkle lightly with salt and line with the rolled out pastry. Trim off the excess and roll out again to make the pie lid. Push in the filling until the plate is full. Cover with a pastry lid.

Place a flat, greased baking sheet over the pie plate and flip upside down. Remove the pie plate, seal the edges of the pastry and make a hole in the centre of the pie. Roll some leftover pastry into an 8cm long worm and place around the hole. Put the pie into the fridge to rest for 30 minutes.

Preheat the oven to 180°C/350°F/gas mark 4.

Bake the pie in the oven for 30 minutes. Allow to cool, then place into the fridge and chill for 2 hours.

After 2 hours, take a funnel and place into the central hole of the pie. Slowly pour 4 tablespoons of the remaining concentrated ham stock into the pie, then chill again. As the stock hits the cold pie filling, it will form a jelly and set. Continue to do this until you can get no more stock into the pie – think of it like a pork pie.

ED'S TIP: A pie plate (which is essentially a deep, enamel plate, a bit like a camping plate) costs very little and are great for making pies – go for a 25cm one. Otherwise, just use a ceramic pie dish.

Steak and kidney pudding

An all-time British classic – of course the name 'pudding' derives from the fact it's being cooked in a pudding basin. It's a fantastic winter warmer; this is true comfort food. Serve with veg and a meat gravy.

SERVES 2

225g self-raising flour, plus extra for dusting
salt and pepper
110g shredded suet
350g stewing steak, cut into small chunks
100g kidneys (ideally lambs' kidneys), cut into small chunks
2 tablespoons flour
50g field mushrooms, sliced

To make the suet pastry, sift the flour and ½ teaspoon salt into a bowl. Add the suet, then add a little water at a time, mixing together to make a stiff paste.

Roll out two thirds of the pastry on a floured surface and use to line a greased 750ml pudding basin. Roll the steak and kidneys in some seasoned flour and put into the basin with the sliced mushrooms. Add 2 tablespoons cold water. Roll out the rest of the pastry on a floured surface and cover the pudding. Cover with greaseproof paper or foil, and steam for 3 to 3½ hours.

Beef and mushroom pie

SERVES 4

400g mushrooms
150ml vegetable oil
50g butter
1 onion, chopped
2 carrots, chopped
900g chuck beef
1 tablespoon flour, plus extra for dusting
2 tablespoons Worcestershire sauce
2 tablespoons fresh thyme leaves
1 tablespoon English mustard
120ml ale
225g puff pastry (see page 226)
1 egg, beaten
400ml beef stock (see page 230)

For the filling, fry the mushrooms in half the oil until softened, then drain on kitchen paper. Add the butter to the pan and gently sweat the chopped onion and carrots until cooked but not coloured.

Add the beef and flour to the pan and brown. Tip in the softened mushrooms, then add the Worcestershire sauce, thyme, mustard and ale. Simmer for 1½ hours on a low heat without a lid.

Remove from the heat and allow to rest for 5 minutes.

Preheat the oven to 220°C/425°F/gas mark 7.

On a floured surface, roll out the pastry to 5mm thick. Pour the filling into a pie dish. Brush the beaten egg around the rim of the dish. Top with the pastry and crimp the edges down. Make a hole in the pie lid and decorate with excess pastry, then brush with egg. Bake in the oven for 15 to 20 minutes, or until golden brown.

Remove the pie from the oven and allow to cool for a few minutes before serving.

ED'S TIP: I would serve a portion of the beef and mushroom pie with braised onions and courgettes and mashed potato.

Hodgepodge pies

SERVES 6–8

3 tablespoons olive oil

300g veal fillets, cut into chunks

300g pork fillets,cut into chunks

300g lamb fillets, cut into chunks

2 large onions, sliced

4 carrots, cubed

2 tablespoons plain flour

800ml strong veal stock

2 tablespoons Worcestershire sauce

1 tablespoon chopped fresh curly
  parsley

1 tablespoon chopped fresh thyme

1 tablespoon chopped fresh chives

salt and freshly ground black pepper

2 tablespoons pearl barley

400g potatoes, peeled and thinly
  sliced

6 tablespoons grated Cheddar cheese

Preheat the oven to 160°C/325°F/gas mark 3.

Place the oil in a large saucepan, heat over a moderate heat and sauté the meat until lightly browned. Transfer to 6–8 small, individual casserole dishes.

Add the onions and carrots to the pan in which the meat was sautéed and cook until lightly browned. Sprinkle in the flour and stir well. Gradually add the veal stock, stirring to achieve a smooth sauce. Add the Worcestershire sauce and herbs and season with salt and pepper.

Divide the mixture between the individual casserole dishes and sprinkle each with the barley, again dividing between the dishes. Arrange the potato slices on top of each individual dish, slightly overlapping, and cover each with foil before placing in the oven to cook for about 50 minutes.

After 50 minutes, increase the oven temperature to 180°C/350°F/gas mark 4. Remove the foil from the dishes and sprinkle the tops with the grated Cheddar. Continue cooking for another 30 minutes, then remove and serve.

Cold Harbour Lane patties

MAKES 10

2 teaspoons sunflower oil

2 shallots, finely chopped

2 garlic cloves

1 Scotch bonnet chilli, deseeded and
chopped

1 teaspoon fresh or dried thyme
leaves

500g minced beef

3 tablespoons garam masala

½ x 400g tin chopped tomatoes

150ml beef stock (see page 230)

½ teaspoon celery salt

juice of ½ lemon

1 egg, beaten

FOR THE PASTRY

450g wholemeal flour

2 tablespoons turmeric

1 teaspoon salt

225g cold butter, cubed

2 eggs, beaten

Heat the oil in a frying pan, add the shallots and fry for a few minutes until softened. Stir in the garlic and chilli and cook for 3 minutes, then add the thyme. Add the mince and garam masala and cook for 10 minutes, stirring occasionally until the meat is browned. Add the tomatoes and beef stock and simmer for 30 minutes until the meat is tender and most of the liquid has been absorbed. Season with the celery salt and stir in the lemon juice. Set aside to cool for 30 minutes.

Meanwhile, make the pastry. Put the wholemeal flour, turmeric, salt and butter into a bowl. Work into crumbs using your fingertips. Add the beaten eggs and gently blend to form a dough. Wrap in clingfilm and chill for 10 minutes.

Preheat the oven to 200°C/400°F/gas mark 6.

Cut the pastry in two and roll out each piece on some greaseproof paper. Stamp out 10 rounds using a saucer. (You'll need to reroll the trimmings to make 10).

Put a generous spoonful of the mince mixture on one half of a pastry round, leaving a border around the edge. Brush the edges with water, then fold the pastry over the mince. Press the edges together to seal and mark with a fork. Cut a couple of holes in the top and repeat with the remaining pastry rounds.

Lift on to a greased baking tray and brush with beaten egg to glaze. Bake for 25 minutes until the pastry is golden, the base is firm and the filling is piping hot.

Folk roast chicken pie

SERVES 4

225g puff pastry (see page 226)

1 whole chicken

100g butter

4 tablespoons olive oil

6 garlic cloves, peeled

250ml single cream

sprig of fresh rosemary, finely
  chopped

6 fresh sage leaves or ½ teaspoon
  dried sage

½ teaspoon salt

¼ teaspoon freshly ground black
  pepper

2 celery sticks, finely chopped

2 large leeks, thoroughly rinsed and
  finely sliced

4 small shallots, cut in half length
  ways

200g button mushrooms, sliced

1 heaped tablespoon flour, plus extra
  for dusting

1 teaspoon green peppercorns

1 glass white wine

400ml chicken stock (see page 230)

1 bay leaf

1 egg, beaten

Roll out the puff pastry on a floured surface to 28 x 20cm and 5mm thick. Place on a tray or large plate and rest in the fridge for 30 minutes.

Joint the chicken into drumsticks and thighs, the breasts cut into four pieces on the bone and the backbone of the chicken cut into two pieces. (Ask your butcher to do this for you.)

Heat half the butter and 2 tablespoons olive oil in a casserole pot, add the chunks of chicken and garlic cloves and brown on all sides so you get a rich brown colour. Now pour over 200ml cream, bring to a gentle simmer and continue to cook for 20 minutes. The cream will split and separate to flavour the chicken and tenderise it.

After 20 minutes, add the chopped rosemary, sage leaves and salt and pepper. Continue to cook, stirring gently for a further 10 minutes before turning off the heat and covering. Leave to rest and cool.

Preheat the oven to 190°C/375°F/gas mark 5.

In a saucepan, heat the remaining olive oil and butter. Add the celery, leeks and shallots and place on to a moderate heat to cook gently for 10 minutes. Now add the mushrooms and cook until lightly coloured. Add the flour and green peppercorns and cook the flour until it gets to a straw colour. Pour in the glass of wine, stirring to avoid lumps forming. Add the chicken stock and a bay leaf. Bring this mixture to a rolling simmer and cook for 10 minutes. Remove from the heat. Set aside to cool for 30 minutes.

Pull chunks of chicken off the bones and add to your sauce mixture with the garlic cloves. Add the remaining cream. Pour the cooled mixture into a 24 x 18cm earthenware pie dish. Moisten the edges of the dish with a little water, lay the pastry over and pinch to seal around the edge. Brush the pastry with beaten egg. Place into the oven. After 5 minutes turn the temperature down to 180°C/350°F/gas mark 4, and after 20 minutes turn the temperature down to 170°C/330°F/gas mark 3½ before cooking for a further 15 minutes.

Remove and serve with vegetables and spoonful of folk music.

Chicken, leek, mushroom and walnut pie

SERVES 4

3 small leeks, thoroughly rinsed

vegetable oil

knob of butter

225g button mushrooms, sliced

75g walnuts, chopped

225g streaky bacon, chopped

150g flour, plus extra for dusting

salt and freshly ground black pepper

4 chunky chicken breasts, cut into
  large cubes

pinch of grated nutmeg

1 bay leaf

½ teaspoon finely chopped fresh
  thyme

300ml chicken stock (see page 230)

2 tablespoons double cream

100g Shropshire blue cheese

350g shortcrust pastry (see page
  223)

1 egg, beaten

FOR THE DRESSING

50g butter

bunch of fresh mint, finely chopped

2 tablespoons olive oil

1 teaspoon Dijon mustard

Slice the leeks in half lengthways. Thoroughly wash them and cut into chunks. Add 1 tablespoon of oil and the butter to a deep-sided frying pan and fry the leeks gently. Once they start to soften, add the mushrooms, cook until softened and then add the walnuts. Pour the contents of the pan into a bowl, and set aside.

Now add a little more oil to the pan and place back on the heat. Fry the bacon until lightly coloured, then remove the pan from the heat. Season the flour with a little salt and pepper. Toss the chicken pieces through the seasoned flour, bring the bacon back up to heat and add the chunks of floured chicken with 1 extra tablespoon of seasoned flour. Fry this mixture until lightly browned, then add the leeks, mushrooms and walnuts back to the pan with grated nutmeg and black pepper. Add the bay leaf and thyme, remove from the heat and add 150ml chicken stock. Put back on to the heat and gently stir together to thicken. Add the remaining stock, bring up the heat and allow to simmer for 20 minutes on a low heat, stirring constantly. If there seems too little stock, add a further 100ml water. As you cook the mixture, it will tend to thicken.

Remove from the heat, season with salt and pepper and add the double cream and Shropshire blue. Set aside to cool for 30 minutes.

Remove the pastry from the fridge and roll out on a floured surface. Line a pie dish. Trim away the excess pastry from the edge and brush the base and all the edges of the pastry with beaten egg. Roll out a further piece of pastry using your trimmings to make a pie lid. Ensuring the pie filling has completely cooled, spoon into the pastry, cover with the lid and trim off the excess pastry. Pinch the pastry together to seal the pie. With a sharp knife, make a small hole in the top to allow the steam to escape, brush with the remainder of the beaten egg and place in the fridge to rest for 30 minutes.

Preheat the oven to 180°C/350°F/gas mark 4. Cook the pie in the oven for 30 minutes.

Make a little dressing by gently melting the butter in the pan. Remove from the heat and add the chopped mint. Whisk the mustard and oil together and whisk into the butter and mint.

Allow the pie to rest for 5 minutes, then serve with a drizzle of the mustard dressing. Accompany with seasonal vegetables if you like.

ED'S TIP: I always try to use free-range chicken and eggs.

Creamy chicken and ham pie

This is great with fresh seasonal vegetables.

SERVES 4

450g chicken thighs and legs

pinch of salt

1 teaspoon white wine vinegar

1 bay leaf

bunch of fresh curly parsley, stalks
   reserved, leaves chopped

75g butter

1 large leek, thoroughly rinsed and
   cut into 2cm chunks

1 onion, cut into 2cm chunks

2 large carrots, cut into 2cm chunks

50g flour, plus extra for dusting

½ teaspoon mustard powder

½ teaspoon mace

¼ teaspoon celery salt

¼ teaspoon white pepper

600ml chicken stock (see page 230)

25ml double cream

175g good quality ham, cut into 3cm
   chunks

350g shortcrust pastry (see page
   223)

1 egg, beaten

Place the chicken thighs and legs in a pot (ideally use a boiler), mix in the salt, vinegar, bay leaf and parsley stalks and pour over 1.8 litres water. Bring up to heat, but do not boil, and poach the chicken for 1 hour. Remove from the heat and allow to cool.

Melt the butter in a pan over a gentle heat, add the vegetables and cook for 5 minutes. Add the flour, cook for a further 2 minutes, then add the mustard powder, mace, celery salt and pepper. Now ladle in the chicken stock a little at a time and add the chopped parsley. Once all of this is combined, cook over a moderate heat for 30 minutes. Remove from the heat, add the cream and allow to cool.

At this point, strip the chicken from the bones and add to the vegetables and cream with the chunks of ham. Pour the filling into a bowl, lay a sheet of clingfilm over the surface and chill in the fridge for 30 minutes.

Preheat the oven to 170°C/330°F/gas mark 3½.

Roll out the pastry on a floured surface to a thickness of 5mm and use to line a pie dish. Trim away the excess pastry and roll out to create a lid. Fill with the chicken and ham mixture and brush the edges of the pastry with the beaten egg. Cover the filling with the pastry lid and pinch the edges together. Brush the surface with more egg wash, make a hole in the top and chill for 30 minutes.

Bake the pie in the oven for 40 minutes.

Shepherd's pie

SERVES 4

75g butter

2 tablespoons vegetable oil

1 large onion, finely chopped

2 carrots, finely chopped

3 celery sticks, finely chopped

2 garlic cloves, finely chopped

100g button mushrooms, sliced

1 tablespoon chopped fresh rosemary

350g minced lamb neck

1 teaspoon tomato purée

1 tablespoon flour

200ml ruby port

1 bay leaf

salt and freshly ground black pepper

600ml lamb or beef stock (see page 230–1)

pinch of mace

FOR THE TOPPING

800g potatoes

300ml hot milk

35g butter

50ml double cream

pinch of nutmeg

Heat the butter and oil in a large saucepan. Add the vegetables, garlic and mushrooms and soften. Add the rosemary and mince and cook until lightly coloured. Add the tomato purée and flour. Cook for 2 minutes, then add the port, bay leaf and seasoning. Turn the heat up, add the stock and mace, and simmer for 1 hour, stirring occasionally.

Pour the mixture into a large oven dish, allow to cool and place in the fridge for 30 minutes.

Preheat the oven to 170°C/330°F/gas mark 3½.

Boil the potatoes until soft, drain and add back into the pan. Mash with the hot milk, butter and cream. Season and add nutmeg to taste. Smooth over the chilled meat and place in the oven for 45 minutes or until browned.

Beef and oyster pie

SERVES 4

75g lard, plus extra for greasing

500g shortcrust pastry (see page 223)

450g beef rump or stewing steak, cut into 2cm cubes

2 level tablespoons flour, plus extra for dusting

1 teaspoon celery salt

2 carrots, finely chopped

2 small onions, finely chopped

small bunch of fresh curly parsley, finely chopped

400ml Guinness

250ml beef stock (see page 230)

2 tomatoes, finely chopped and lightly salted

1 tablespoon malt vinegar

¼ teaspoon Tabasco

2 x 85g tins smoked oysters in sunflower oil

1 egg, beaten

Lightly grease a 25cm enamel pie plate (see tip page 122) with lard. Roll out the pastry on a floured surface and line the pie plate. Trim off the excess, then roll out the remaining pastry to make a lid for the pie. Put both in the fridge to rest for 30 minutes.

Heat 50g of the lard in a large casserole pot until smoking. Add the beef and fry until lightly browned, then add the flour and the celery salt. Brown for a further 2 minutes then remove to a plate and set aside.

Now add the chopped vegetables and the remaining lard and cook over a gentle heat for 5 minutes. Return the beef to the casserole and add the parsley, Guinness, beef stock, salted tomatoes, vinegar and Tabasco. Cook over a low heat for 50 minutes, stirring every 10 minutes.

Remove the casserole from the heat, and pour into a deep-sided tray to cool for 30 minutes. Once

cooled, gently fold in the strained smoked oysters.

Preheat the oven to 170°C/330°F/gas mark 3½.

Spoon the mixture into the pastry-lined enamel plate. Brush the edges of the pastry with beaten egg. Cover with the lid and pinch the edges together. Make a hole in the top and brush the pastry with beaten egg. Place into the oven to cook for 45 to 50 minutes. Remove from the oven, allow to rest for 5 minutes and serve.

ED'S TIP: A traditional Victorian way of serving the pie is not to brush the pastry with egg but to remove the pie from the oven after 35 minutes of cooking, cover the pie with a flat baking tray and flip the pie upside down. Turn the oven up to 190°C/375°F/gas mark 5, brush what has now become the top of the pie with beaten egg and cook for a further 10 minutes. Our Australian and New Zealand cousins call this a pie floater!

Game pie

This recipe makes enough filling to fill two 30cm pie dishes. You can either make two pies and freeze one for later use or freeze half the filling. Great served with Savoy cabbage and buttered parsley potatoes.

SERVES 8

1 pheasant, boned and cut into cubes

1 pigeon breast, boned and cut into cubes

1 rabbit, boned and cut into cubes

1 large duck breast, cut into cubes

275g venison haunch or best braising venison, cut into cubes

100g flour, plus extra for dusting

3 tablespoons oil

75g butter

1 large onion, sliced

4 rashers of smoked streaky bacon, chopped

2 large field mushrooms, sliced

900ml chicken stock (see page 230)

½ bottle dry red wine

100ml ruby port

½ teaspoon chopped fresh rosemary

½ teaspoon chopped fresh thyme

1 bay leaf

1 mushroom or vegetable stock cube

salt and freshly ground black pepper

1kg shortcrust pastry (see page 223)

1 egg, beaten

milk

Preheat the oven to 150°C/300°F/gas mark 2.

Toss the pheasant, pigeon, rabbit, duck and venison chunks in 75g of the flour. Heat the oil and a knob of the butter in a pan and brown the meat in batches, then remove and place in a casserole dish.

In a frying pan, melt the remaining butter and brown the onion and bacon. Drop in the mushrooms and cook for 3 minutes. Add the remaining flour and cook until brown.

Heat the stock, wine, port, fresh herbs and bay leaf in a separate pot. Add the stock cube and check the seasoning. Add this mixture to the onion and bacon mixture, stirring in the flour to form a smooth, thickened stock. Add this to the casserole dish, stir and cover. Place in the oven and cook for 2 hours.

Remove the casserole dish from the oven and transfer the contents to a large bowl. Allow to cool.

Turn the oven temperature up to 200°C/400°F/gas mark 6.

Roll out the pastry on a floured surface to 5mm thick and use to line the pie dishes, trimming away the excess. Roll out the remaining pastry to create lids for the pies. Brush the edges of the pie dishes with beaten egg and spoon in the pie filling. Cover with the remaining pastry, trim the edges and either pinch or press down with the tines of a fork to seal. Brush the top of the pastry with milk and place in the fridge to rest for at least 30 minutes.

Bake in the oven for 15 minutes, then reduce the temperature to 180°C/350°F/gas mark 4 and cook for a further 15 minutes.

Rabbit, monkfish and savoy cabbage pie

I thought of this recipe while I was walking along the coast of Dartmouth. The two main ingredients, one deep below the ocean and the other leaping around the woods, seem to have a synergy. This feeling comes from my experience of fishing in the morning and catching a monkfish and then checking traps from the night before, foraging through the woods for mushrooms and combining it all with some home-grown cabbage. For me, the fish and the rabbit have a natural affinity, the flavours and textures of monkfish and rabbit really complementing each other.

SERVES 4

4 tablespoons plain flour, plus extra
   for dusting

salt and white pepper

1 whole rabbit, jointed and boned, cut
   roughly into 3cm pieces (keep the
   bones for stock)

75g butter

½ Savoy cabbage (or 1 small Savoy
   cabbage), yellow leaves only, cut
   into small chunks

6 small shallots, chopped (keep the
   skins for stock)

150g chestnut mushrooms, sliced

1 teaspoon white wine vinegar

bunch of fresh tarragon, leaves
   chopped (keep the stalks for stock)

1 teaspoon English mustard

150ml milk

2 bay leaves

900g monkfish tail, filleted (keep
   the bones for stock), cut into 4cm
   pieces

100ml double cream

100g shortcrust pastry (see page
   223)

1 egg, beaten

FOR THE STOCK (OR USE 750ML CHICKEN STOCK,
   SEE PAGE 230)

bones of 1 rabbit

1 bay leaf

fresh tarragon stalks

green leaves from ½ Savoy cabbage
   (or 1 small Savoy cabbage),
   chopped

skins of 6 shallots

bones of 900g monkfish tail,
   chopped

Make the rabbit and monkfish stock. Thoroughly
rinse the rabbit bones, place in a pot and cover with

cold water. Add the bay leaf, tarragon stalks and
chopped cabbage leaves, shallot skins and monkfish
bones. Bring to the boil, immediately turn tot the
lowest heat and simmer for 20 minutes. Remove
from the heat and allow to cool.

Mix the flour with ½ teaspoon white pepper and
¼ teaspoon salt. Dust the pieces of rabbit in
seasoned flour. In a large casserole dish, melt half
the butter and sear the chunks of rabbit until golden
brown. Remove from the dish and set aside.

Add the remaining butter and gently fry the
cabbage, shallots and mushrooms until they just
start to soften. Add the vinegar and stir. Now add 2
tablespoons of the seasoned flour, left over from
dusting the rabbit, stir through and cook for 2
minutes. Tip in the pieces of rabbit and add the
tarragon, and start to ladle in the stock, stirring
gently all the time. Do not allow to boil as this will
make the rabbit tough.

Once you've added all the stock, add the
mustard, milk, and the bay leaves. Cook over a
gentle heat for 15 minutes, remove from the heat
and stir in the pieces of monkfish and the cream.
Pour into a large earthenware dish, set aside and
allow to cool.

Roll out the shortcrust pastry on a floured
surface until 3mm thick. Ensuring the rabbit and
monkfish filling has cooled, lay the pastry over the
dish. Crimp the edges and trim the excess pastry.
Brush with the beaten egg wash and place into the
fridge to rest for 30 minutes.

Preheat the oven to 170°C/330°F/gas mark 3½.
Cook the pie in the oven for 40 to 45 minutes.

ED'S TIP: Serve the pie with mashed carrots.

Tandoori roast chicken

I'm not serving this with any rice – it tastes so good you'll easily get through half a chicken! But, if you fancy it, serve with basmati rice on the side.

SERVES 4

2 whole spring chickens (about 1kg each), jointed into legs and breasts
2 tablespoons lemon juice
1 tablespoon crushed garlic
1 tablespoon grated fresh ginger
1 teaspoon salt
1 teaspoon chilli powder
50g butter, melted
4 tablespoons vegetable oil
1 lime
1 teaspoon chaat masala

FOR THE SPICED YOGHURT MARINADE

250g thick yoghurt
1 teaspoon garam masala
100ml vegetable oil
½ teaspoon ground cinnamon
½ teaspoon chilli powder
1 teaspoon salt

FOR THE SALAD

½ fresh coconut, flesh shaved
bunch of fresh coriander, chopped
1 red onion, sliced
100g beetroot leaves
1 frisée lettuce
2 tomatoes, chopped

FOR THE DRESSING

1 teaspoon cumin seeds
juice of 2 limes
2 tablespoons olive oil
pinch of chilli powder
pinch of salt
pinch of sugar
1 teaspoon chopped fresh ginger

Preheat the oven to 180°C/350°F/gas mark 4.

Make 2–4 deep incisions in each piece of chicken without cutting right through the flesh, then place into a shallow dish. Mix the lemon juice with the garlic and ginger, salt and chilli powder. Spread all over the chicken pieces and leave to marinade for 5 minutes.

Mix together the ingredients for the spiced yoghurt marinade. Coat the chicken with the marinade and leave for a further 5 minutes.

Place the chicken on a rack in a roasting tray and roast in the oven for 25 to 30 minutes.

Take the chicken out of the oven and baste with the butter and oil. Return to the oven and cook for a further 10 minutes or until the chicken is cooked. Remove and leave to rest on the rack for 5 minutes.

Meanwhile, mix all the salad ingredients together in a bowl.

For the dressing, toast the cumin seeds in a pan on the hob for 1 minute, until they start to crackle. Allow to cool lightly before crushing in a pestle and mortar. Add the remaining dressing ingredients, mix together and toss with the salad.

Serve the chicken on individual plates with a squeeze of lime juice and accompanied by the chaat masala and the salad.

Chicken tikka masala

I believe this is the most British of all curries as it was, in fact, invented in England. It is the most popular curry across the country as it has a mild flavour.

SERVES 4

1kg chicken, cut into pieces

2 cups basmati rice

25g butter

½ cucumber, deseeded and finely chopped

300ml yoghurt

1 teaspoon mint sauce (see page 235)

handful of fresh coriander leaves, to serve

1 tomato, finely chopped, to serve

1 lime, cut into wedges, to serve

FOR THE MARINADE

3 tablespoons natural yoghurt

1 teaspoon lemon or lime juice

1 teaspoon turmeric

1 teaspoon chilli powder

1 teaspoon ground coriander

1 teaspoon ground cumin

1 teaspoon grated fresh ginger

1 garlic clove, crushed

salt

FOR THE TIKKA MASALA PASTE

1-2 tablespoons olive oil

1 onion, finely chopped

2.5cm piece of fresh ginger, grated

2 garlic cloves, crushed

1 teaspoon chilli powder

1 teaspoon ground coriander

1 teaspoon ground cumin

4 tablespoons tomato purée

3 tablespoons double cream

Mix together the marinade ingredients. Coat the chicken pieces with the marinade and place in the fridge for 1 hour.

Cook the rice in 4 cups of salted water. Once all the water has been absorbed by the rice, turn off the heat and stir in the butter. Pop the lid back on and leave to one side.

For the tikka masala paste, heat the oil in a large, wide, lidded pan and fry the onion over a medium heat until brown. Add the ginger and garlic and sauté, then add the spices and cook for 30 seconds. Stir in the tomato purée and 1 teaspoon salt and simmer for 1 to 2 minutes.

Add the marinated chicken to the paste in the pan. Stir and cook, covered, for 10 to 15 minutes on a medium heat. Add the cream and gently stir for 3 to 5 minutes.

To make a dip, mix the cucumber with the yoghurt and mint sauce.

Spoon the chicken tikka masala in the middle of individual plates with the rice around it. Serve with coriander leaves, chopped tomato, lime and a dollop of the yoghurt dip.

Mixed vegetable curry

SERVES 4

vegetable oil

25g butter

1 aubergine, halved lengthways

1 small butternut squash, peeled,
  deseeded and cut into thin wedges

3 carrots, halved lengthways

salt and freshly ground black pepper

200ml vegetable stock (see page
  231)

2 onions, finely sliced

pinch of sugar

200g peas

200g soya beans

1 broccoli stem, cut into florets

1 x 400ml tin coconut milk

2 cups basmati rice

FOR THE GREEN CURRY PASTE

bunch of fresh coriander

2 garlic cloves

1 teaspoon chaat masala

2 teaspoon garam masala

2 shallots

½ teaspoon chilli powder

5 cardamom pods

1 teaspoon cumin seeds

thumb-sized piece of fresh ginger

Place all the green curry paste ingredients in a food processor and blitz until you have a smooth paste. Place to one side.

Cut the aubergine halves each into 8 long pieces.

In a large non-stick frying pan, heat a splash of oil and the butter over a moderate heat. Add the squash and aubergine and fry for 5 minutes.

Scoop the curry paste into the pan and cook for 2 minutes. Drop in the carrots, add a pinch of salt and pour over the vegetable stock. Bring to the boil, turn to low heat and simmer for 20 minutes.

Pour 400ml vegetable oil into a sturdy saucepan. Heat the oil to 160ºC/325ºF using a cooking thermometer. Alternatively, drop a clove of garlic into the oil, and when it starts to fizz, the oil is at the right temperature. Remove the garlic clove.

Stir the onions into the hot oil. Place a sieve over a saucepan. Once the onions are a dark brown colour, gently pour the contents of the pan into the sieve to drain the onions. Place the pan with the hot oil to one side and allow to cool.

Drain the onions on kitchen paper. Sprinkle with the sugar and a pinch of salt – this side dish is known as 'tobacco onions'.

Once the curry has been cooking for 20 minutes, add the coconut milk, peas, soya beans and broccoli. Bring to a gentle boil, and then turn down to a simmer.

Meanwhile, bring 4 cups of water to the boil. Add the rice, half a teaspoon of vegetable oil and a pinch of salt. Cover with a tight-fitting lid and place over a high heat. Once the water comes back to the boil, turn down to a low heat and allow the rice to simmer for 10 minutes – do not uncover the pan during this time. Once all the water has been absorbed and the rice is cooked, turn off the heat. Fluff the rice up with a fork, cover and leave to stand for 5 minutes.

Now taste the curry for seasoning and give it a good stir. Serve along with the rice and the onions.

Lamb chops in a fiery Masala sauce

Combining the finest lamb in the world with delicious spices and gentle cooking, this has to be one of the best supper dishes around.

SERVES 4

16 lean, trimmed lamb chops, cut 2cm
   thick
1 tablespoon chilli powder
salt and freshly ground black pepper
50g butter
½ teaspoon chilli powder
pinch of turmeric
pinch of ground cumin
pinch of ground coriander
1 tablespoon natural yoghurt
3 fresh green chillies, deseeded and
   chopped
2 cinnamon sticks
5 whole cloves
3 bay leaves
2 cardamom pods
5 dried plums (Kashmiri if you can
   find them)
2 onions, chopped
1 whole garlic bulb, cloves separated
50g tomatoes
handful of fresh coriander leaves, to
   serve
lime and lemon wedges, to serve

Beat the lamb chops with a mallet to tenderize them, then place in a dish. Sprinkle all over with the chilli powder and season with salt and pepper. Place in the fridge and leave for 2 hours.

Purée the onions in a blender, add the garlic cloves and continue to purée. Remove from the blender and set aside.

Blanch the tomatoes for a few seconds in boiling water, then peel and purée.

Heat a little of the butter in a frying pan and fry the chops until golden brown. Remove the chops to a plate to rest.

Add the remaining butter to the frying pan with the onion and garlic purée and sauté on a moderate heat until transparent. Add the chilli powder, turmeric and a splash of water so that the spices don't burn. Pour in the puréed tomatoes, sauté for a couple of minutes, then add the cumin and coriander and season to taste.

When the butter and the sauce start to separate, stir in the yoghurt.

Place the chops back in the pan and cover with the masala sauce. Add the green chillies, cinnamon stick, cloves, bay leaves and cardamom pods to the pan with the plums. Cover with a lid and simmer gently for 10 minutes until the chops are tender.

Serve the chops garnished with fresh coriander and wedges of lime and lemon.

Spicy prawn Malai with alu mash

SERVES 4

4 large Madagascan prawns, cleaned and peeled

½ tablespoon turmeric

salt

squeeze of lemon juice

vegetable oil

sugar, to taste

2 small onions, finely chopped

4–5 garlic cloves, mashed to a paste

2 tomatoes, finely chopped

1 tablespoon chilli powder

2 fresh green chillies

1 tablespoon English mustard

1 x 400ml tin coconut milk

2 sprigs of fresh coriander, chopped

FOR THE ALU MASH

3 large potatoes, peeled and cut into chunks

200ml milk

50g butter

salt and freshly ground black pepper

3 spring onions, finely chopped

1 tomato, finely chopped

1 tablespoon cumin seeds

FOR THE ENGLISH MUSTARD DRESSING

3–4 teaspoons English mustard

1 tablespoon honey

1 teaspoon lemon juice

6 tablespoons olive oil

Boil the potatoes for the alu mash in salted water for 20 minutes.

Meanwhile, put the prawns in a bowl, add a pinch of turmeric, a little salt and a squeeze of lemon juice and leave to rest for 5 minutes.

Heat 1 tablespoon of oil in a pan and fry the prawns for 1 minute. Remove from the heat and set the prawns aside on a plate to rest.

Add some more oil to the frying pan, add a touch of sugar and heat gently. Add the onions and garlic. Cook for a minute, then add the tomatoes, remaining turmeric and chilli powder. Cook for a few minutes on a moderate heat until you have a paste and the oil is released.

Add the prawns and green chillies. Stir for a minute, then add the mustard and coconut milk. Add salt to taste and a little water. Cover and cook for 2–3 minutes. Just towards the end, add the fresh coriander.

Drain the potatoes and mash with the milk and half the butter until light and fluffy. Season to taste. Melt the remaining butter in a frying pan and add the spring onions. After 1 minute, add the tomato and cumin seeds and toss for a minute or so. Add the mashed potato and mix thoroughly. Season to taste and remove from the heat.

For the dressing, mix the mustard, honey, lemon juice and olive oil together in a bowl.

Serve the prawn malai with the alu mash and dressing and a garnish of curly lettuce.

Caribbean chicken curry

SERVES 4–6

salt

1 tablespoon white wine vinegar

1 boiling chicken, cut into pieces

1 head of garlic, broken into cloves
    and chopped

75g mild Madras curry powder

vegetable oil

1 teaspoon cumin seeds

3 potatoes, peeled and sliced

2 tablespoons coconut cream

2 chicken stock cubes

3 cups basmati rice

FOR THE SPICE MIXTURE

1 tablespoon curry powder

2 teaspoons cumin seeds, toasted

2 teaspoons dried thyme

bunch of spring onions, finely
    chopped

1 teaspoon garlic powder

3 bay leaves

½ teaspoon turmeric

1 tablespoon southern spice mix (see
    page 91) or jerk seasoning

juice of 1 lemon

FOR THE ROTI

500g bread flour, plus extra for
    dusting

250g self-raising flour

1 teaspoon salt

1 tablespoon baking powder

1 litre vegetable oil

FOR THE RAITA

½ cucumber, deseeded and cut into
    cubes

1 onion, sliced

250ml natural yoghurt

Mix half a teaspoon of salt with the vinegar in a large bowl until the salt has dissolved. Soak the chicken pieces for 10 minutes in the mixture.

Mix together all the spice mixture ingredients, half the chopped garlic and a pinch of salt. Remove the chicken from the vinegar and marinate in the spice mixture for 10 to 15 minutes. Meanwhile, make the roti dough. Mix the flours, salt and baking powder in a large bowl. Stir in enough warm water to form a dough. Cover with a tea towel and leave to rise for 10 to 15 minutes.

Mix the Madras curry powder with a little water to form a paste. Heat 3 tablespoons of vegetable oil in a large lidded pan. Add the cumin seeds, the remaining garlic and the curry paste. Cover and cook on a moderate heat for 2 to 3 minutes. Add the chicken and spice mix, replace the lid and reduce the heat. Cook for 20 minutes, adding a little water if it looks too dry.

Add the potatoes, coconut cream and stock cubes, cover and cook for a further 30 minutes. For the raita, mix the onions, cucumber and yoghurt together in a bowl.

Cook the rice for 10 minutes in a 12 cups of salted, boiling water. Drain well, place back in the pan and keep warm.

Cut the roti dough into 12 pieces, dust in bread flour and roll into thin circles. Pour the vegetable oil into a deep-sided saucepan. Heat the oil to 160°C/325°F using a cooking thermometer. Alternatively, drop a clove of garlic into the oil, and when it starts to fizz, the oil is at the right temperature. Remove the garlic clove.

Cook the roti for 2 seconds in the hot oil, then flip over and cook for another couple of seconds. Drain on kitchen paper. Repeat until you have cooked all 12 rotis.

Serve the curry accompanied by the rice, the roti folded into triangles and the raita on the side.

Aromatic green chicken curry

SERVES 4

vegetable oil, for greasing

4 small sweet potatoes, peeled and
  cut into 2cm slices

25g butter, melted, plus 2
  tablespoons

100g fresh coriander, roughly
  chopped

100g fresh fenugreek leaves, chopped

6 spring onions, chopped, plus extra
  to serve

5 fresh hot red chillies, chopped

4 garlic cloves, roughly chopped

2 teaspoons grated fresh ginger

1 teaspoon cumin seeds

3 tablespoons Greek yoghurt, plus
  extra to serve

1 chicken, boned and cut into 3cm
  dice

1 teaspoon garam masala

1 teaspoon turmeric

1 teaspoon salt

100ml double cream

100g brown shrimps, peeled

Preheat the oven to 180°C/350°F/gas mark 4. Grease a baking tray and line with tinfoil.

Brush the sweet potatoes with the melted butter, place on the prepared baking tray and bake for 40 minutes.

Place the coriander, fenugreek, spring onions, chillies, garlic and ginger into a blender and blitz to a paste.

In a large, deep frying pan, toast the cumin seeds over a moderate heat, then add 2 tablespoons of the melted butter, the coriander paste and a dash of yoghurt. Cook until the fat floats on top of the mixture. Add the chicken, garam masala, turmeric, salt, the remaining yoghurt and the cream and cook for 10 minutes on a low heat. Add the shrimps and cook for a further 1 minute.

Mix the curry and baked sweet potatoes and serve with chopped spring onions and yoghurt.

Swanage Bay sea bream with anchovy butter

SERVES 2

2 lemons

2 x 275g sea bream, gutted and
  scaled

salt

4 large sprigs of fresh rosemary,
  leaves finely chopped

1 tin anchovies, drained

1 garlic clove

75g butter, cubed

100g flour

2 tablespoons olive oil

Preheat oven to 120°C/250°F/gas mark ½. Zest one of the lemons, place the zest to one side and halve the lemon.

Make deep slits in the fish at 3cm intervals. Squeeze the juice of half a lemon over the fish, massaging it into the meat and slits. Sprinkle with a little salt. Allow to rest.

To make the anchovy butter, put the rosemary into a pestle and mortar with the anchovies and garlic. Mash into a paste. Add the lemon zest and butter. Squeeze in the lemon juice from the remaining half. Work together to form a light, fluffy, flavoured butter.

On a large tray, mix the flour with some salt and pepper. Coat the fish in this mixture. Heat the oil over a moderate heat in a frying pan. Cook the fish for 5 minutes on either side.

Cut two wedges out of the remaining lemon. Serve the bream with a spoonful of flavoured butter and a wedge of lemon.

ED'S TIP: The ideal partners for this dish are boiled new potatoes and buttered runner beans.

Creamy fish pie

SERVES 4–6

1 carrot, chopped

1 celery stick, chopped

450ml whole milk

10 black peppercorns

1 small onion, chopped

zest of 1 lemon

1 bay leaf

1 whole nutmeg, grated

150g salmon

150g cod fillet

150g naturally smoked haddock fillet

2 large eggs

500g floury potatoes, such as King
   Edwards

50g butter

75ml double cream

12 raw tiger prawns

FOR THE SAUCE

75g butter

50g plain flour

75ml double cream

bunch of fresh parsley, finely
   chopped

100g strong Cheddar cheese, grated

Dijon mustard, to taste

white pepper

Place the carrot and celery in a pan with the milk, peppercorns, onion, lemon zest, bay leaf and nutmeg. Add the salmon, cod and haddock. Poach gently for 10 minutes.

In another pan, hard-boil the eggs then allow to cool. Turn the heat under the poaching pan off, cover with a lid and leave until the fish is cool enough to flake. Sieve the milk and set aside.

Boil the potatoes until cooked, then drain them and mash with the butter and cream.

To make the sauce, melt the butter, add the flour and cook for 3 to 4 minutes. Gradually add the cream, poaching milk, parsley and half the cheese. Add mustard and white pepper to taste and cook for 5 to 7 minutes.

Peel the boiled eggs. Remove the sauce from the heat and flake in the fish and add the prawns. Place the fish and sauce in an ovenproof 20 x 25cm casserole dish with the hard-boiled eggs.

Pipe or spoon the mashed potato on top and top with the remaining cheese over the top. Bake the dish for 20 to 25 minutes at 180°C/350°F/gas mark 4 until golden brown.

Take the fish pie out of the oven and leave to rest a little. Scoop out a hearty spoonful on to a plate.

ED'S TIP: This pie goes really well with some wilted spinach and roasted vine tomatoes on the side. Place the tomatoes on a roasting tray with a drizzle of olive oil and roast for 15 minutes and, just before serving, wilt the spinach in a pan for a minute.

Poached haddock

SERVES 2

1 onion, halved

500ml whole milk

1 bay leaf

450g smoked haddock fillet

10 new potatoes, sliced

salt and freshly ground black pepper

200ml double cream

1 tablespoon wholegrain mustard

small bunch of fresh chives, finely
  sliced

25g butter

200g spinach, washed

Place the onion halves, milk and bay leaf in a large frying pan on a moderate heat. Allow the milk to come to a gentle simmer. Cut the haddock fillet in half to make two portions. Place skin side up into the pan, cover with tinfoil and poach for 5 minutes.

Cook the potato slices in boiling, salted water for 5 minutes.

Remove the haddock with a fish slice to a plate. Cover with the tinfoil.

Pour the poaching liquid through a sieve into a clean saucepan and place back on the heat. Stir in the cream, then add the mustard, chives and a good pinch of pepper. Simmer for 3 to 4 minutes.

Drain the potatoes and add them to the saucepan. Gently stir.

Melt the butter in a frying pan over a moderate heat and cook the spinach for 1 minute until wilted.

Divide the spinach on to two plates. Using a slotted spoon, scoop the potatoes out of the sauce and arrange over the spinach. Now peel the skin away from the haddock and place the haddock on top of the potatoes. Finish with a drizzle of sauce.

ED'S TIP: You can top the fish with a poached egg if you like.

Scallop and bacon skewers

SERVES 2

250g spinach

1 garlic clove, crushed

50g butter

50ml double cream

2 tablespoons good-flavoured
  Cheshire cheese, grated

salt and freshly ground black pepper

1 tablespoon breadcrumbs

olive oil

4 slices of streaky smoked bacon

4 chunks of crusty bread

4 large diver-caught scallops

FOR THE SAUCE

1 teaspoon capers

2 anchovy fillets

a sprig of fresh rosemary, leaves
  picked

150ml tomato passata

50g pine nuts, toasted

1 lemon, cut into wedges

Preheat the oven to 180°C/350°F/gas mark 4.

To make the sauce, heat 2 tablespoons olive oil in a pan. Add the capers, anchovies and rosemary. Stir in the tomato passata and finish with the pine nuts and lemon wedges and cook for 20 minutes.

Meanwhile, fry the spinach with the garlic in the butter. Add the cream, cheese and season. Place in a small ovenproof dish and sprinkle over the breadcrumbs. Cook in the oven for 15 minutes.

Roll the bacon around the chunks of bread and thread them on to skewers, alternating with the scallops. Drizzle with olive oil, season and grill on a griddle on all sides until cooked. If you don't have a griddle, cook under a hot grill instead.

To serve, slide the scallops and bread chunks off the skewers on to a big plate. Spoon over some of the sauce and serve with the spinach on the side.

Halibut with creamy fennel and potato bake

SERVES 4

600ml fish stock (see page 230)

juice of 1 lemon

25ml Noilly Prat

3 star anise

small bunch of fresh oregano, leaves
  picked

2 tablespoons flour

salt and freshly ground black pepper

4 x 200g halibut fillets

vegetable oil

knob of butter

200g green beans, topped and tailed,
  and blanched

25g butter

1 tablespoon chopped fresh mint

1 tablespoon vinegar

1 teaspoon wholegrain mustard

FOR THE FENNEL AND POTATO BAKE

250g new potatoes, sliced

1 large bulb of fennel, finely sliced

300ml double cream

100g strong Cheddar cheese, grated

Preheat the oven to 170°C/330°F/gas mark 3½.

To make a glaze, put the fish stock, lemon juice, Noilly Prat and star anise in a small saucepan. Reduce by four fifths over a moderate heat. Add the oregano.

Place the new potatoes and fennel together in a pan of boiling water and cook for 5 minutes. Drain, then mix with the cream, cheese and some seasoning. Scoop into an ovenproof earthenware dish. Cover with tinfoil and cook in the oven for 20 minutes.

Mix the flour with some salt and pepper. Lightly dust the pieces of halibut in the seasoned flour.

Heat 2 tablespoons of vegetable oil with the knob of butter in a frying pan. Pan-fry the halibut fillets for 2 minutes on each side. Turn off the heat then pull the fillets on to their sides in the pan and allow to rest for 1 minute.

Meanwhile, gently heat the beans with the butter, mint, vinegar and mustard.

Serve the fish with the creamy fennel and potato bake, the minted beans and the reduced fish glaze poured over.

Baked cod steak with a cheese crust

SERVES 4

4 x 175g thick cod steaks

1 teaspoon English mustard

1 tablespoon olive oil

1 shallot, finely chopped

1 garlic clove, finely chopped

10 tomatoes, peeled, deseeded and
  chopped

½ teaspoon sugar

2 tablespoons white wine

salt and freshly ground black pepper

butter, for greasing

1 shallot, chopped

150ml chicken stock (see page 230)

150ml Noilly Prat

150ml double cream

50g cold butter

salt and freshly ground black pepper

2 tablespoons chopped fresh parsley

FOR THE CHEESE CRUST

100g white breadcrumbs

2 tablespoons chopped fresh parsley

100g Wensleydale cheese, grated

50g unsalted butter

salt and freshly ground black pepper

Preheat the oven to 200°C/400°F/gas mark 6. Brush one side of the fish with mustard. Put to one side.

Heat the oil in a wide pan, then sweat the shallot and the garlic in the oil, but don't colour them. Add the tomatoes, sugar and white wine. Cook to a paste – this takes about 10 minutes – season and put to one side.

Meanwhile, to make the cheese crust, blend the breadcrumbs and parsley together in a processor. Add the cheese and butter, blend and season. Spread out on a tray and freeze for 40 minutes. Grease an ovenproof dish with a little butter.

Cut the cheese crust into 4 rectangles - the same size as the cod steaks. Place the fish mustard side up and spread over a layer of the tomato paste. Carefully lay a rectangle of cheese crust on top of each cod steak. Place into the greased ovenproof dish with the chopped shallot, chicken stock and Noilly Prat.

Bake the fish for about 6 or 7 minutes, then take out and rest.

Pour the stock from the tray into a hot pan and reduce by two thirds. Add the cream and reduce again, until it is the thickness of a sauce. Beat in the butter and season. Strain into a clean pan and stir in the parsley.

To serve, place the fish in the middle of a plate and spoon the sauce around.

ED'S TIP: Braised new potatoes, green beans and broccoli are perfect on the side.

Monkfish with tomato, chorizo and pea concassé

SERVES 2

1 teaspoon ground cumin

1 teaspoon celery salt

1 teaspoon dried oregano

200g monkfish

olive oil

1 tablespoon natural yoghurt

1 tablespoon pesto

FOR THE CONCASSÉ

½ onion, chopped

50g chorizo, sliced

½ fresh red chilli, deseeded and
 chopped

1 garlic clove, chopped

½ Little Gem lettuce, cut into wedges

2 tablespoons Pernod

2 tablespoons white wine

100ml fish stock (see page 230)

1 large tomato

60g peas

knob of butter

small bunch of fresh marjoram, leaves
 chopped

Mix together the cumin, celery salt and oregano. Coat the fish all over in this spice mix.

Begin the concassé. Heat some more olive oil and soften the onion for 1 minute. Add the chorizo, chilli and garlic and fry for a further minute before adding the lettuce, Pernod and white wine to the pan. Flambé before adding the fish stock. Bring to the boil and reduce by half.

Meanwhile, score the tomato with an 'x' on its bottom. Immerse in boiling water for 10 seconds before dunking it in iced water. Peel off the skin and cut in half crossways. Hold the tomato halves in your hand, cut side down, and squeeze to rid them of their seeds and water. Dice the tomato flesh and set aside.

Cook the peas in boiling water and set aside. Heat some olive oil in a pan and fry the monkfish for 5 minutes, turning it once.

Fold the butter and marjoram into the concassé pan with the chorizo, chilli and onion. Lastly, add the peas and tomato and remove from the heat.

Combine the yoghurt and pesto in a bowl.

Slice the monkfish and serve on top of the tomato, chorizo and pea concassé, with the pesto sauce on the side.

Caspian's lobster linguine

My son Caspian's favourite… Savour the lovely
flavours with a glass of chilled white wine.

SERVES 4

1 x 750g live lobster

salt and freshly ground black pepper

50ml olive oil

1 onion, finely chopped

1 carrot, finely chopped

1 celery stick, finely chopped

2 garlic cloves, finely chopped

2 anchovy fillets

75ml white wine

400ml tomato passata

zest and juice of ½ lemon

200ml fish stock (see page 230)

500g linguine

6 basil leaves, chopped

Kill the lobster by driving a knife down into the
cross mark on its head. Boil the lobster in salted
water for 10 minutes. Drain and leave to cool.

Put the lobster on a tea towel. To cut it half
lengthways, insert a knife into the head and push
down through the head and the tail. Then turn the
lobster round and split the rest of the head.

Remove the meat from the tail to a plate. Crack
the claws with the back of a knife and remove all the
meat. Add to the tail meat on the plate. Make sure
you retain the body shell but not the claws.

Wipe the board clean to avoid any fragments of
shell getting into the sauce, then thinly slice the
lobster meat. Place back on the plate and chill.

Pour half the olive oil into a 5-litre (or larger)
saucepan. Add the vegetables and garlic and stir-fry
on a moderate heat for 3 minutes. Stir in the
anchovies. Now add the reserved lobster shell and
fry for 1 minute.

Pour in the wine and reduce by half. Add the
tomato passata, bring to the boil and gently simmer
for 10 minutes. Add the lemon zest, juice and fish
stock and continue to simmer for 10 minutes.

Bring 4 litres of salted water to the boil and cook
the pasta, stirring occasionally, for 8 minutes. Drain.

Remove the lobster shell from the sauce. Season,
then stir in the remaining olive oil, sliced lobster
meat, basil and drained pasta. Toss thoroughly
and enjoy.

Skate with shrimps and capers

Skate has to be one of my all-time favourite fish, but for some strange reason, most people haven't adopted it as one of their favourites. Yes, it has long, thin, plastic-like bones, running through the wing and it can have a slight ammonia smell, but once cooked, it is easy to eat and delicious. Nearly 90 per cent of all skate caught off the British coast is exported to our more knowledgeable continental cousins. The southwest of England has an abundant, sustainable supply of this fish. Serve with new potatoes and crisp green British vegetables.

SERVES 4

50g semolina

25g plain flour

salt

4 x 250g skate wings, trimmed and
   skinned

100g butter

1 tablespoon capers

1 tablespoon finely chopped parsley

100g brown shrimps

juice of 1 lemon

On a large tray, combine the semolina and flour with a good pinch of salt. Lightly rinse the skate wings, dry them on kitchen paper and then coat liberally with the flour and semolina mixture.

Preheat the oven to 180°C/350°F/gas mark 4. Line an oven tray with tinfoil and place in the oven – this is to keep the skate warm (you'll only be able to cook two at a time, so you'll need to keep the first two hot while cooking the other two).

Heat a 30cm frying pan to a moderate heat. Melt half the butter until it starts to bubble. Add two of the skate wings to the pan. Gently cook the fish for 4 minutes. Turn over each skate wing and cook for a further 4 minutes.

Remove the fish and place on to the preheated oven tray and keep warm in the oven. Cook the other two wings, adding the remaining butter to the pan and repeating the process. Once you've finished cooking all four skate wings, place them on to individual plates. Now add the capers and parsley to the pan, shake gently. Toss in the brown shrimps and finish with lemon juice.

Remove from the heat and gently spoon the shrimps, capers and juices over the skate wings.

Crispy fried cod with lentils

SERVES 4

2 egg whites

8 tablespoons whipping cream

4 x 100g boneless cod fillets

1 litre vegetable oil, for deep-frying

2 teaspoons chopped fresh parsley

1 lemon, cut into wedges

FOR THE LENTILS

100g Puy lentils, rinsed in lots of
   cold water

700ml chicken or vegetable stock
   (see page 230-1)

1 teaspoon salt

2 tablespoons finely diced onion

2 tablespoons finely diced carrot

2 tablespoons finely diced leek

2 tablespoons finely diced celery

2 tablespoons finely diced potato

6 tablespoons sherry vinegar

100g cold unsalted butter, diced

FOR THE SPICED FLOUR

8 tablespoons plain flour

4 tablespoons baking powder

1 teaspoon cayenne pepper

1 teaspoon dried thyme

1 teaspoon white pepper

1 teaspoon garlic pepper

1 teaspoon salt

To cook the lentils, place them with the stock and the teaspoon of salt in a small pan. Bring to the boil and simmer for 10 minutes. Add the diced vegetables and cook for a further 5 minutes. Strain through a fine sieve into a saucepan. Add the vinegar and whisk in the diced butter. Keep warm.

Whisk the egg whites until they have a shaving foam consistency and mix with the cream. Sift the ingredients for the spiced flour together into a shallow bowl. Run the cod fillets through the spiced flour, then dip them into the cream mixture. Run them through the flour again. Repeat if you prefer a slightly thicker crust.

Pour the vegetable oil into a deep-sided saucepan – make sure it doesn't come any higher than halfway up the side of the pan as the level will rise once you lower in the fish. Heat the oil to 160°C/325°F using a cooking thermometer. Alternatively, drop a clove of garlic into the oil, and when it starts to fizz, the oil is at the right temperature. Remove the garlic clove.

Preheat the oven to 120°C/250°F/gas mark ½. Place your plates in the oven to warm up, plus a baking tray lined with tinfoil. Carefully place two cod fillets into the hot oil and cook for about 4 minutes, until they are crisp and golden. Drain on kitchen paper. Keep warm on the tray in the oven while you cook the remaining fillets.

To serve, spoon generous amounts of lentils on to your warmed plates and top with a cod fillet. Finish with a sprinkling of parsley and a wedge of lemon.

Southern fried mackerel with coleslaw

SERVES 4

2 potatoes

salt

15g southern spice mix (see page 91)

8 mackerel fillets

vegetable oil

100ml milk

1 x apple compote recipe (see page 232)

FOR THE COLESLAW

½ red cabbage, finely grated

1 large carrot, grated

1 large onion, grated

juice of ½ lemon

2 tablespoons mayonnaise

pinch of cayenne pepper

pinch of salt

Boil the potatoes in salted water for 10 minutes and allow to cool a little. Slice them and, while still warm, sprinkle them with a little of the spice mix. Pan-fry in vegetable oil until golden brown.

Place the remaining spice mix in a shallow bowl, and the milk in another shallow bowl. Run the mackerel fillets through the spice mix, then through the milk and then back through the spice mix. Pan-fry on both sides until golden brown.

Mix all the coleslaw ingredients together. Divide the coleslaw and potatoes on to four plates and top each plate with two mackerel fillets. Finish off with apple compote and serve.

Poached turbot and clam saffron stew

Homemade hollandaise sauce is the perfect accompaniment to this simple but special dish.

SERVES 2

olive oil

2 shallots, finely sliced

1 garlic clove, chopped

100g podded fresh peas

100ml white wine

400ml fish stock (see page 230)

150g palourde clams

2 x 200g turbot steak

pinch of saffron

small bunch of fresh parsley, finely chopped

FOR THE HOLLANDAISE SAUCE

1 egg yolk

100g butter

salt and freshly ground black pepper

juice of ¼ lemon

1 teaspoon white wine vinegar

Heat a little oil in a large saucepan and gently soften the shallots and garlic. Add the peas and white wine and bring to the boil. Pour in the fish stock and gently lower in the clams and turbot. Sprinkle in the saffron and cook gently for 5 minutes or until cooked.

To make the hollandaise sauce, blitz the egg yolk with 1 tablespoon water in a blender. Melt the butter and, when bubbling, pour slowly into the blender with the motor running. Season to taste and then stir in the lemon juice and the vinegar.

Serve the turbot and clams in a bowl or deep plate and pour over the saffron liquor. Sprinkle with parsley and serve the hollandaise sauce on the side.

Apricot and raspberry scones

When we made these scones for the photograph, the team just couldn't eat enough of them. The trick here is to ensure you add the raspberries right at the end and be extremely delicate once they're in the dough. Lovely served with a cup of tea, clotted cream and bramble jelly.

MAKES 10–12

50g dried apricots

225ml milk

500g self-raising flour, plus extra for dusting

30g baking powder

85g butter, cut into small cubes, plus extra for greasing

85g sugar

50g raspberries

1 egg, beaten

Preheat the oven to 200°C/400°F/gas mark 6.

Put the dried apricots in the milk and allow to soak. Sift the flour and baking powder into a large bowl. Add the sugar and butter and mix with your hands.

Slowly add the apricots and milk until it comes together to form a dough. Gently work the dough until smooth, making sure not to overwork it.

On a floured surface, roll out the dough to 4cm thick. Scatter the raspberries over half the dough, fold over the other half and then carefully roll it out again so the fruit is in the middle. Lightly flour a round cutter and stamp out circles. Glaze with the beaten egg.

Grease a baking tray and dust with flour. Put the dough circles on the baking tray and bake in the middle of the oven for 20 minutes until golden brown.

Sweet loaf

This is a large loaf, but it is extremely moreish and you will find that it disappears quite quickly.

MAKES 1 LOAF

1kg plain flour, plus extra for dusting
600ml mineral water
10g yeast
60ml unsalted butter, plus extra for
  greasing
3 large eggs
20g salt
120ml honey

In a food processor, combine the flour, water and yeast together (see tip) and work it with a dough hook. As it starts to form a dough, add the butter, eggs, salt and honey. Continue to work into a smooth dough for at least 5 minutes.

Dust a large surface with flour. Cut the dough into three balls. Using your hands, roll the balls into 40cm cylinders. Lay the cylinders side by side and plait together.

Cover a baking tray with greaseproof paper. Grease with a little butter and sprinkle with flour. Place the loaf on to the baking tray, dust with flour and cover loosely with clingfilm. Allow to rise for 1½ hours.

Preheat the oven to 190°C/375°F/gas mark 5. Bake the loaf for 35 to 45 minutes.

ED'S TIP: Alternatively, you can use 250ml starter (see page 208), 250ml mineral water and 5g yeast.

Scotch pancakes

These are delicious with bacon, a fruit-based cream or a rich jelly or jam (see the jellies and marmalades on pages 232–5 for some ideas)

SERVES 2

100g self-raising flour
25g caster sugar
1 egg, beaten
150ml milk
1 tablespoon vegetable oil

Place the flour and sugar into a bowl. Make a well in the middle, add the beaten egg and half the milk. Beat until it forms a thick batter, then whisk in the remaining milk.

Place a frying pan over a moderate heat and pour in the oil. Add 1 tablespoon of the batter and cook until bubbles form on the top, then flip it on to the other side and cook for 30 seconds. Lay the pancakes on a tea towel and cover with another tea towel to keep soft.

Rum, sultana and nut bread

MAKES 1 LOAF

250ml golden rum

75g sultanas

400g strong wholemeal flour

110g strong white flour, plus extra for
dusting

25g fresh yeast or 1 packet dried
yeast

10g salt

75g walnuts

50g flaked almonds

Pour the rum into a saucepan. Add the sultanas, bring to the boil and boil for 2 minutes. Remove from the heat and allow to cool.

Mix both flours, the yeast, salt and cooled rum/sultanas in a bowl until it all becomes a soft and pliable dough.

Place the dough on a lightly floured flat surface and knead for 5 minutes. Alternatively, use the dough hook in a food processor – this is far easier. Put the worked dough back in a bowl and cover loosely with clingfilm. Leave in a warm place to rise for an hour.

Preheat the oven to 200°C/400°F/gas mark 6.

Bring out the dough and mix in the walnuts and almonds. Mould the dough into a loaf shape. With a sharp knife, slit down the centre of the loaf.

Allow to rest on a floured baking tray for 30 minutes, then place in the centre of the oven and bake for 30 minutes until browned. Remove from the oven and cool on a wire rack.

Gingerbread

MAKES 1 LOAF

100g margarine

175g black treacle

50g golden syrup

150ml whole milk

2 eggs, beaten

225g plain flour

50g sugar

1 teaspoon mixed spice

1 level teaspoon bicarbonate of soda

2 teaspoons ground ginger

oil or butter, for greasing

Preheat the oven to 155°C/310°F/gas mark 2½.

Place the margarine, treacle and syrup into a large saucepan and warm up. Add the milk and allow to cool.

Blend the eggs with the cooled mixture. Sift the flour, sugar, spice, bicarbonate of soda and ground ginger into a large bowl. Scoop the mixture from the saucepan into the bowl and blend in with a metal spoon.

Grease an 18 or 20cm baking tin, 2.5cm deep, and line with greaseproof paper. Fill with the gingerbread mixture. Bake on the middle shelf of the oven, for 1¼ hours if using an 20cm tin, or 1½ hours if using a 18cm tin.

Pound cake

An old-fashioned favourite, so called because traditionally it was made with one pound of everything and about eight eggs! I've halved the amounts and there's still more than enough to satisfy the whole family and still have some to keep.

MAKES 1

225g butter, plus extra for greasing

225g sugar

4 eggs

110g sultanas

110g currants

zest of 1 large lemon

50g candied peel

2 tablespoons brandy

225g plain flour, sifted

½ teaspoon salt

Preheat the oven to 170°C/330°F/gas mark 3½.

Cream the butter and sugar together until light and fluffy. Add the eggs one at a time, beating well after each addition.

Add the sultanas, currants, lemon zest, candied peel and brandy. Stir in gently.

Fold in the sifted flour and salt using a metal spoon. Grease a 20cm round cake tin, line with greaseproof paper and scoop in the cake mixture. Bake for 2½ to 3 hours.

Fairy cakes

The Hummingbird Bakery in London has made a small fortune out of recreating these humble cakes. They're delicious plain or with icing.

MAKES 24

110g margarine or butter, softened
110g caster sugar
½ teaspoon vanilla extract
2 eggs
225g self-raising flour
4 tablespoons whole milk

FOR THE BUTTER-CREAM ICING (OPTIONAL)
50g butter
275g icing sugar, sifted
½ teaspoon vanilla extract

Preheat the oven to 190°C/375°C/gas mark 5.

In a mixer, beat the butter or margarine to a soft cream, gradually adding the sugar until it is smooth and fluffy. Beat in the vanilla extract.

Add the eggs, one at a time, beating in a tablespoon of flour before adding the second egg. Now stir in the remaining flour, mixing well. Add the milk a tablespoon at a time until a smooth consistency is achieved.

Line a baking tin with fairy cake cases and fill each one two thirds full with the cake mixture. Bake in the oven for 15 to 20 minutes.

Cool on a wire rack.

For the icing, beat all the icing ingredients together until creamy and spoon a little on top of each cake.

Fruit cake

Just the thing with a hot cup of tea.

MAKES 1

450g dried mixed fruit
1 level teaspoon bicarbonate of soda
75g softened butter, plus extra for
  greasing
175g sugar
1 egg
275g self-raising flour
4 drops almond essence
3 tablespoons rum
1 tablespoon demerara sugar

Preheat the oven to 180°C/350°F/gas mark 4. Grease a 20cm cake tin.

Place the mixed fruit into a saucepan, add just enough water to cover and boil for 5 minutes. Remove from the heat and allow to cool, then add the bicarbonate of soda.

Beat the butter and sugar together until light and fluffy, then add the egg. Continue to whisk, then fold in the flour, almond essence and the cooled fruit. Pour the mixture into the cake tin and bake for 1 hour.

Turn down the oven to 130°C/275°F/gas mark 1 and leave the cake in the oven for a further 1½ hours. Remove from the oven, drizzle with the rum and dust with the demerara sugar.

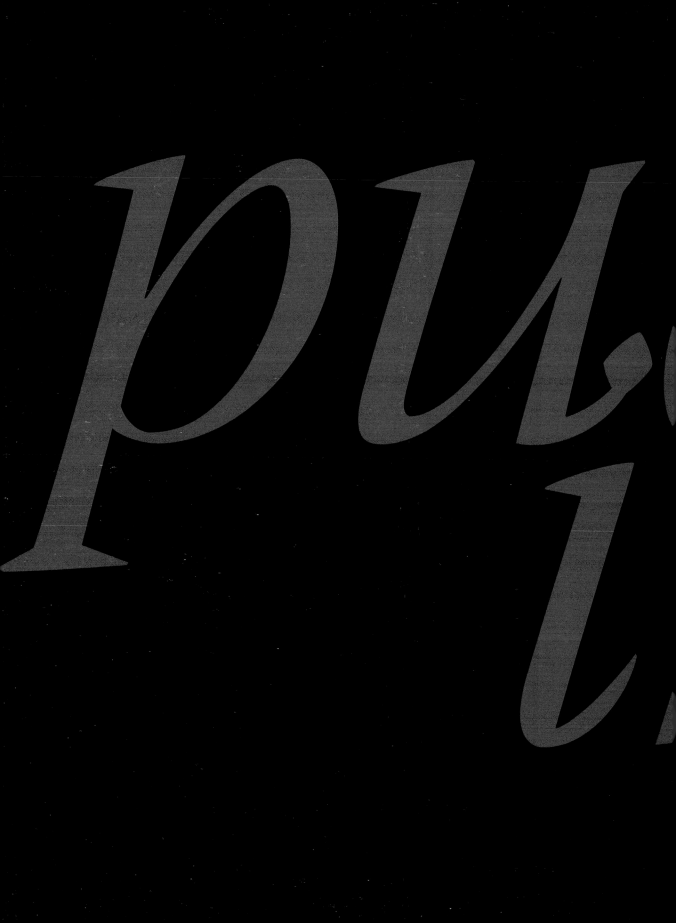

Steamed blueberry syrup sponge pudding

I think syrup sponge pudding, with a drizzle of fresh custard and a spoonful of cream is my all-time favourite English pud. I've altered the traditional recipe slightly by adding blueberries – I like the way they pop in your mouth as you eat the hot pudding.

SERVES 4

50g unsalted butter, softened

75g caster sugar

2 whole eggs

100g plain flour

1 tablespoon baking powder

2 tablespoon whole milk

150g blueberries

oil or butter, for greasing

golden syrup, to serve

custard, to serve (see page 195)

Cream the butter and sugar together thoroughly. Ensure that the butter turns a nearly white colour before you add the eggs (if you don't do this the pudding will not rise properly).

Sift in the flour and baking powder and fold into the butter and sugar mixture. Add the milk and gently fold in the blueberries– try not to split them.

Grease a pudding basin. Pour in the mixture. Cover with greaseproof paper with a fold in the centre of the paper to allow the pudding to expand. Cover loosely with foil, and make a hole in the centre. Tie the greaseproof paper around the rim with a piece of string.

Place the pudding in a steamer or a saucepan (ensure it has a firm-fitting lid) with water coming up to 2cm from the top of the pudding basin. Cover and steam for 1 hour or boil for 45 minutes.

Carefully remove the pudding basin from the pot. Remove the greaseproof paper and foil. Run a small knife around the edge of the pudding basin to break the air lock and ensure that the pudding slides out smoothly. Place a dish over the pudding basin and flip it over, then lift off the pudding basin. Pour over large quantities of golden syrup and serve with custard.

ED'S TIPS: You can use any berries you like in this recipe. You can even try adding small chunks of chocolate or grated fresh marzipan to the batter.

As an alternative to golden syrup, serve with warmed jam or a drizzle of maple syrup.

Frangipane and blackberry tart

SERVES 6

225g English blackberries

25ml kirsch

400g sweet pastry (see page 223)

flour, for dusting

2 medium eggs

50g caster sugar, plus extra for
  dusting

50g icing sugar

100g salted butter

100g ground almonds

25g flaked almonds

clotted cream, to serve

Soak the blackberries in the kirsch. Preheat the oven to 180°C/350°F/gas mark 4.

Roll out the pastry on a floured surface and line a 25cm tart tin with it. Line the pastry case with greaseproof paper and fill with baking beans. Bake the pastry blind for 20 minutes. Remove from the oven and leave to stand. Leave the oven on.

Meanwhile, make the filling. Mix the eggs, caster sugar, icing sugar and butter with a hand blender until fluffy. Add the ground almonds and stir thoroughly. Pour the filling mix into the tart case and push down the whole blackberries into the mixture. Top with the flaked almonds and a dusting of caster sugar.

Bake for 30 minutes. Remove and allow to cool.

Serve a good wedge of the tart with a dollop of clotted cream.

Eton Mess

SERVES 4

4 egg whites

275g caster sugar

½ teaspoon vinegar

250g strawberries, hulled

150g raspberries (or any other berries
  you can find)

400ml double cream

50g sugar for cream mixture

Preheat the oven to its lowest setting.

Line a baking tray with greaseproof paper. Get yourself a bowl that is spotless clean and drop in the egg whites and 2 tablespoons of the sugar. Start whisking the whites with an electric mixer (making sure the mixer is clean, too).

After 2 minutes, start adding the remaining sugar a little at a time, reserving 50g of the sugar for later. Keep mixing until you work this mixture into a thick glossy consistency – the most common mistake when making meringues is undermixing the mixture.

Fold the vinegar gently through the mixture. Now blob large spoonfuls of meringue mixture on to the greaseproof paper.

Bake in the oven for 2 to 3 hours, then remove and allow the meringue to cool.

Cut the strawberries into quarters. Whisk the double cream and remaining sugar until just peaking – don't overwhisk it. Now fold the berries into the cream and refrigerate.

When the meringues are cool, break them into chunks and place into a large bowl. Pour the cream and berry mixture over the meringues and gently fold together.

To serve, scoop the Eton Mess into large glasses.

Apple and plum crumble with ripple ice cream

SERVES 4

3 Granny Smith apples, peeled, cored
  and diced
150g golden caster sugar
200g butter, plus extra for frying
150g plain flour
50g hazelnuts, chopped

FOR THE ICE CREAM

500ml double cream
500ml semi-skimmed milk
1 vanilla pod
150g golden caster sugar
10 egg yolks

FOR THE RIPPLE

500g plums, stoned
150g golden caster sugar
juice of 1 lemon

To make the ice cream, heat the cream, milk, vanilla pod and 1 tablespoon of sugar in a pan. Using an electric whisk, whisk the egg yolks and the remaining sugar together, then slowly whisk in the hot milk mix. Strain the ice-cream mixture into a pan and heat gently until it coats the back of a spoon. Transfer to a bowl and chill for 30 minutes.

To make the plum ripple, heat the plums with the sugar, lemon juice and 100ml water until the fruit breaks down. Using a hand blender, blitz the hot plum mixture. Pour half into a bowl and refrigerate for 20 minutes; keep the other half at room temperature.

Preheat the oven to 180°C/350°F/gas mark 4.

Coat the apples in the sugar then pan-fry them in butter. For the crumble topping, blend the butter, sugar and flour in a food processor until it forms a crumble. Add the pan-fried apples to the bowl of unchilled ripple sauce and pour the mixture into ramekins. Top with the crumble mixture. Place the crumbles in the oven for 20 minutes.

Pour the ice-cream mixture into an ice cream machine and churn it for 20 minutes.

Stir the chilled half of the ripple into the ice cream and churn briefly. Transfer to the freezer. Sprinkle the hazelnuts over the crumbles and continue to bake for a further 5 minutes.

Serve the crumbles in their ramekins with a spoonful of the ice cream on the side.

Rhubarb bread and butter pudding

Try to source your cream and milk for this recipe from a local farm if you can – the flavour will be so much richer.

SERVES 6

1kg rhubarb, washed and cut into 2cm
  lengths
150g vanilla sugar (see tip), plus
  extra for dusting
500ml milk
500ml double cream
pinch of salt
1 vanilla pod, seeds scraped out
4 eggs
170g caster sugar
butter, plus extra for greasing
pinch of salt
1 loaf soft white bread, sliced

FOR THE CINNAMON AND VANILLA ICE CREAM

1 cinnamon stick
500ml milk
1 vanilla pod, split
500ml cream
10 egg yolks
225g caster sugar

To make the ice cream, whiz the cinnamon stick in a blender until roughly ground. Place the milk in a pan with the ground cinnamon and the split vanilla pod and seeds. Bring slowly to the boil, add the cream and leave to cool and infuse for about 25 to 30 minutes.

Whisk the egg yolks and sugar until pale and fluffy. Then add the milk, cream, cinnamon and vanilla mixture and whisk together. Pour back into the pan and heat gently until the mixture just coats the back of a wooden spoon.

Pass the mixture through a sieve into a large plastic container. Then place it in a sink full of iced water. Pour into an ice-cream machine and churn for 40 minutes until set.

Meanwhile, place the rhubarb in a pan with the vanilla sugar and gently cook for about 15 minutes until starting to soften and the juices are running.

Remove the rhubarb from the heat and, together with its juices, put it in a sieve over a bowl. Allow to drain and leave to stand for about 30 minutes to cool. The strained juices will be used for a coulis.

Combine the milk and double cream. Add a pinch of salt, the vanilla seeds and the pod. Bring to a gentle boil then set aside to allow the vanilla to infuse for 10 to 15 minutes.

Preheat the oven to 170°C/330°F/gas mark 3½.

Beat the eggs and caster sugar until pale and fluffy. Pass the milk and cream mixture through a sieve into the egg and sugar mixture. Stir together.

Butter a large square or rectangular dish (about 24 x 24 x 5cm) and start by placing a thin layer of rhubarb on the bottom.

Butter slices of bread, remove the crusts and cut into triangles then place butter side down on top of the rhubarb, slightly overlapping as you go to create a single layer. Repeat with a layer of rhubarb on top of the bread and then a bread layer, but place it butter side up this time.

Ladle the cream mixture carefully over the layers until it fills the dish to the top. Leave to stand for at least 30 minutes.

Place the dish in a large roasting tray, half filled with boiling water. Dust the surface with vanilla sugar and bake in the oven for 25 minutes.

To make the rhubarb coulis, pour the drained rhubarb syrup into a saucepan and cook over a medium heat until reduced by half. Allow to cool.

ED'S TIP: Keep used vanilla pods and push into a bag of sugar to make vanilla sugar.

Sticky toffee and date pudding

I would serve this delicious pudding with a dollop of crème fraîche.

SERVES 6

100g chopped dates

½ teaspoon vanilla extract

35g softened butter, plus extra for greasing

65g demerara sugar

1 egg, beaten

1 teaspoon black treacle

75g self-raising flour

½ teaspoon bicarbonate of soda

60ml milk

FOR THE SAUCE

25g butter

75g dark soft brown sugar

120ml double cream

1 tablespoon black treacle

Preheat the oven to 180°C/350°F/gas mark 4.

In a small bowl, soak the dates with the vanilla extract in 100ml boiling water for 5 minutes, then drain and mash.

Cream together the butter and sugar. Mix the egg into the butter mixture, then beat in the treacle.

Fold in one third of the flour and all the bicarbonate of soda. Add half the milk and repeat, continuously adding the milk and flour until it is all used. Then stir in the mashed dates. Spoon the pudding mixture into buttered ramekins and bake for 20 to 25 minutes.

To make the sauce, put the butter, sugar and half the cream in a pan. Bring to the boil and simmer for about 5 minutes until the sugar has dissolved. Stir in the black treacle, turn up the heat and let the mixture simmer for 2 to 3 minutes, stir occasionally. Remove from the heat and stir in the remainder of the cream.

To serve, turn the puddings out on to a plate. Pour the toffee sauce over the top.

Spotted dog with rum and fruit

This differs from the traditional spotted dick recipe, its inspiration coming from the English navy, as you can see from the rather large quantity of dark rum.

SERVES 6

50g currants

50g dried cherries

50g dried plums, chopped

200ml dark rum

zest of ½ lemon

300g plain flour, sifted

10g baking powder

150g suet or vegetarian suet,
  shredded

75g caster sugar

225ml whole milk

butter, for greasing

600ml custard (see page 195)

Soak all the fruits with the rum and lemon zest for 30 minutes.

To make the pudding, mix together the sifted flour, baking powder, suet and sugar in a large bowl. Add the milk to the dry ingredients and combine into a batter.

Pass the soaked fruit through a sieve, reserving the rum liquor for the custard. Fold the fruits through the batter.

Grease a pudding basin with butter and then pour in the batter. Cover with greaseproof paper and a layer of tinfoil. Tie with string. Place the pudding in a steamer or a saucepan with water coming up to 2cm from the top of the pudding basin. Steam for 1 hour or boil for 45 minutes.

Meanwhile, make the custard, adding 2 tablespoons of the reserved rum with the milk and cream to the egg yolk mixture.

Gently remove the pudding basin from the pot. Remove the greaseproof paper and foil. Run a small knife around the edge of the pudding basin to break the air lock and to ensure the pudding slides out smoothly. Place a dish over the pudding basin and flip it over. Lift off the pudding basin.

Serve with the custard.

Chocolate slice

SERVES 4

300g dark chocolate

225g unsalted butter

75g self-raising flour

200g milk chocolate, chopped

175g walnuts, chopped

3 eggs

225g light muscovado sugar

oil or butter, for greasing

TO SERVE

punnet of fresh raspberries

clotted cream

few sprigs of fresh mint leaves

icing sugar, for dusting

Preheat the oven to 190°C/375°/gas mark 5.

Melt the dark chocolate in a heatproof bowl over a pan of simmering water and stir in the butter until melted. Remove from the heat.

Mix the flour with the milk chocolate and nuts.

In a separate bowl, beat the eggs and sugar. Pour the melted chocolate and butter into the egg mixture, beat together and stir in the flour, chocolate and walnut mixture.

Grease and line a baking tin and transfer the mixture to it. Bake in the oven for 30 to 40 minutes. Remove from the oven and leave to cool for 1 hour. Cut into squares and serve with the clotted cream, raspberries topped with mint and a dusting of icing sugar.

Apricot pudding with sponge drops

A simple, traditional set pudding, similar to jelly, but with cream.

SERVES 4

3 eggs, separated

75g caster sugar

1 tablespoon lemon juice

2 leaves ready-to-soak gelatine

150ml double cream

200g apricot purée

FOR THE SPONGE DROPS

2 eggs

50g caster sugar

35g plain flour

13g cornflour

Place a heatproof bowl over simmering water. Put the egg yolks, sugar and lemon juice into the bowl and whisk until thick and creamy.

Dissolve the gelatine in 2 tablespoons of water. Add the egg yolk mixture and whisk until amalgamated. Whip the cream and mix into the egg yolk mixture. Fold in the fruit purée.

Whisk the whites in a clean bowl to form soft peaks. Fold the egg whites into the pudding mixture and place in the fridge to set for 4 hours.

For the sponge drops, start by preheating the oven to 180°C/350°F/gas mark 4. Line a baking tray with greaseproof paper.

Whisk the eggs and sugar until thick and fluffy, then stir in the plain flour and cornflour. Place small spoonfuls of the mixture on to the prepared baking tray and bake for 3 minutes. Allow to cool.

Serve the sponge drops on a plate with a scoop of pudding.

Traditional apple pie

This is an old, old-style apple pie. Lovely served with a dollop of whipped double cream.

SERVES 6

900g Bramley apples, peeled, cored
  and chopped
pinch of salt
2 teaspoons quince marmalade
lemon juice
butter, for greasing
caster sugar

FOR THE PASTRY

175g self-raising flour, plus extra for
  dusting
85g margarine
85g lard
pinch of salt
300ml milk, plus extra for glazing

Until you are ready to use them, put the apples and salt in a bowl of water to prevent them from turning brown.

To make the pastry, sift the flour into a bowl and add the margarine, lard and salt. Cut the mixture with a knife until it is combined. Add the milk, bit by bit, until you have a dough. Do not use your hands, just the knife. The dough should be elastic and not too wet or dry. Chill in the fridge for 30 minutes.

Drain the water from the apples and put them in a pan over a medium heat with the quince marmalade and cook for about 10 minutes. Add the lemon juice and sugar to taste. Set aside to cool.

Dust a surface with flour. Roll out two thirds of the pastry into a rectangular shape. Fold in three by folding each end into the middle. Turn the pastry 90 degrees and roll. Repeat the process of folding and rolling twice more. Keep your rolling movements very light to prevent the pastry from becoming biscuit-like.

Preheat the oven to 210°C/410°F/gas mark 6½.

Grease a 22cm pie plate with butter. Roll out the folded pastry and line the pie plate with it. Cut off the trimmings and reserve for the lid.

Put the apple in the middle of the base, leaving space all around it. Brush the edges of the pastry with milk. For the lid, roll the remaining pastry and trimmings together into a circle large enough to cover the pie. Place it over the pie filling and cut a slash in the pie lid. Go around the edges, lifting and pinching them to seal. Glaze the top with more milk and sprinkle with a little sugar.

Place in the oven for 20 to 25 minutes until the pastry is a rich golden brown. It is important not to undercook the pastry.

Cut a slice of the pie and enjoy.

ED'S TIP: Quantities of the marmalade, lemon juice and sugar will depend on the tartness of the apples used; make sure you taste the filling and adjust any quantities before putting it into the pie.

Homemade Bakewell tart

SERVES 6

400g sweet pastry (see page 223)

butter, for greasing

50g raspberry jam

3 eggs

115g unrefined sugar

115g unsalted butter, melted

115g ground almonds

25g grated marzipan

1 teaspoon Amaretto

50g flaked almonds

Preheat the oven to 180°C/350°F/gas mark 4.

Roll out the sweet pastry and then line a 25cm greased flan ring with it. Cut off the excess pastry and crimp the edges.

Heat the jam with 3 tablespoons of water in a saucepan and press it through a fine sieve. Spread evenly over the base of the tart.

Beat the eggs and sugar together and then slowly fold in the melted butter, almonds, marzipan and Amaretto. Pour into the pastry base. Bake in the oven for about 35 to 40 minutes.

Take out and leave to cool, then cut into large slices and serve.

Custard

MAKES 600ML

1 vanilla pod, split lengthways

300ml whole milk

30ml double cream

3 tablespoons caster sugar

4 egg yolks

Scrape the seeds out of the vanilla pod. Put the milk, cream, vanilla seeds and pod into a small pan and bring to the boil. Remove from the heat.

Put the egg yolks and sugar into a bowl. Whisking constantly, pour in the hot vanilla and cream mixture.

Pour the custard into a heatproof bowl, place over a saucepan of boiling water and stir until thickened. Pour into a serving jug.

Cloutie dumpling

'Cloutie' means 'cloth' in Scots.

SERVES 8

150g self-raising flour, plus extra for
 dusting
150g brown breadcrumbs
150g suet
1 teaspoon bicarbonate of soda
2 teaspoons cinnamon
150g sultanas
100g raisins
100g soft light sugar
2 tablespoons black treacle
1 teaspoon ground ginger
300ml milk

Soak a clean cloth, the size of a tea towel, in boiling water. Mix all the ingredients together to make a fairly soft consistency – make sure everything is mixed well. Take the cloth out of the water and wring, then lay out flat and dredge well with flour. Smooth the flour over the cloth with your hands to get an even spread.

Form the mixture into a ball and place it on the cloth. Draw the cloth together evenly around the dumpling mixture, leaving room for expansion, and tie up with string.

Put a plate in the bottom of a large pot (the pot should be big enough to allow the dumpling to be covered with water – you want enough water to avoid having to top it up during cooking). Place the tied cloth on to the plate in the pan, fill with water and bring to the boil. Turn the heat down and simmer the dumpling for 2 to 3 hours.

Remove the dumpling from the pot and put in a colander in the sink. Untie the string and gently pull the corners of the cloth apart. Put a plate over the dumpling in the colander and turn it over. Carefully pull the cloth off the dumpling.

Preheat the oven to 120°C/250°F/gas mark ½. Place the dumpling, plate and all, on to a baking tray and bake for 30 minutes.

Serve the dumpling with custard (see page 195).

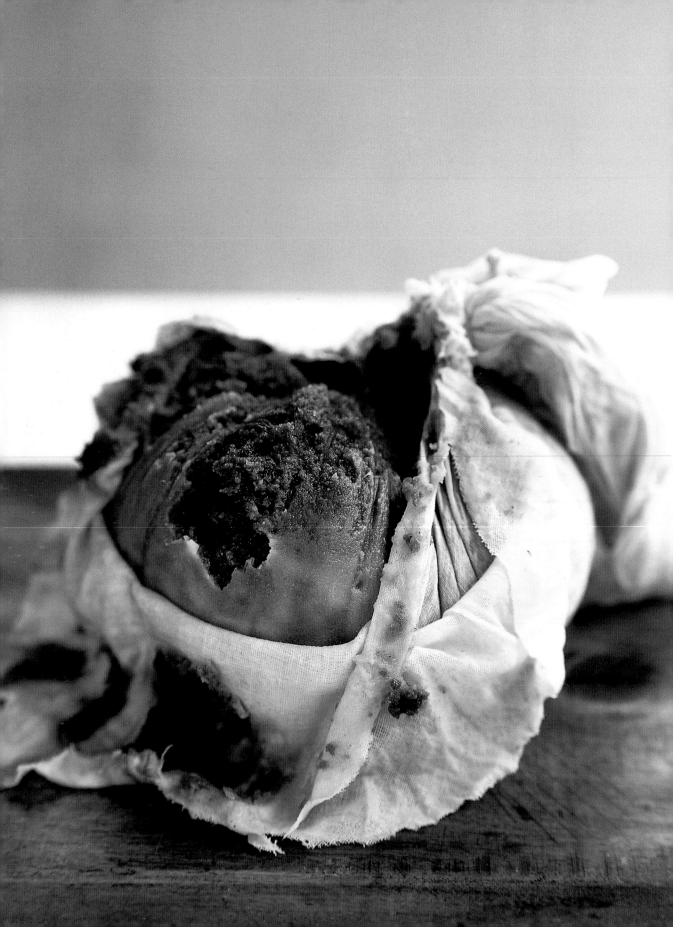

Fruit and nut tart

SERVES 8

25g sultanas

25g raisins

250ml rum

25g butter

35g sugar

1 large egg

25g glacé cherries

25g walnuts, chopped

25g desiccated coconut

FOR THE PASTRY

50g self-raising flour, plus extra for
  dusting

25g butter (goat's butter is really
  nice in this recipe)

1 egg

FOR THE BOOZY CREAM

200ml double cream

2 tablespoons icing sugar

In a bowl, soak the sultanas and raisins in the rum
for 2 hours or overnight.

Preheat the oven to 160°C/325°F/gas mark 3.

To make the pastry, knead together the flour,
butter, egg and 300ml water. Roll out the pastry on
to a floured surface to a 5mm thickness and use it to
line individual 25cm tart tin.

For the filling, melt the butter and sugar together.
Leave to cool. Beat the egg and whisk it into the
cooled butter and sugar mixture. Strain the soaked
raisins and sultanas (reserve the rum) and then mix
them, together with the cherries, walnuts and
coconut, into the butter and sugar mixture.

Spoon the mixture over the pastry case and bake
for 30 to 35 minutes. Whisk the double cream with
icing sugar and the reserved rum.

Serve your tart with a dollop of boozy cream.

Lemon and wild berry tart

SERVES 10

butter, for greasing

about 400g sweet pastry (see page
  223)

zest and juice of 2 unwaxed lemons

4 tablespoons double cream

100g ground almonds

200g sugar

5 eggs

120g butter, melted

100ml Devon apple brandy

handful of blackberries

handful of raspberries

120g butter, melted

icing sugar

clotted cream or Jersey double
  cream, to serve

Grease a 30cm tart tin with butter and then line it
with the sweet pastry. Let it rest in the refrigerator
for at least an hour or overnight.

Preheat the oven to 180°C/350°F/gas mark 4.
Line the pastry with greaseproof paper. Cover the
paper with baking beans and bake for 15 minutes.
Remove from the oven and allow to cool before
removing the paper and the beans.

Put the lemon zest and juice into a large bowl.
Add the cream, almonds, sugar, eggs and butter.
With a hand blender, mix it all together to form a
paste. Stir in the apple brandy. Spread the berries
over the bottom of the pastry and then spread the
creamy lemon mixture on top.

Bake in the oven for about 20 minutes. Allow the
tart to cool slightly but not too much because it
should be enjoyed warm. Decorate it with a thick
layer of icing sugar and serve with clotted cream or
fresh Jersey double cream.

Chocolate rum mousse

This is a classic, cold chocolate mousse recipe that for me, works every time. A very good friend of mine is a true connoisseur of chocolate mousse – he insists on trying every variety in every restaurant he has visited. When he tries this one, I think he'll agree that it's hard to beat.

SERVES 4

175g chocolate

5 egg yolks

1 vanilla pod, seeds scraped out

1 teaspoon instant coffee

250ml double cream

2 tablespoons rum

5 egg whites

Melt the chocolate in the top of a double saucepan over hot, but not boiling water. Remove from the heat and allow to cool a little.

Meanwhile, beat the egg yolks lightly and gradually fold them into the melted chocolate. Add the vanilla seeds. Dilute the coffee in 1 tablespoon of hot water and then fold it into the chocolate mixture.

Beat the cream until thick. Stir in the rum and fold the cream into the chocolate mixture. Beat the egg whites until stiff peaks form and fold into the mixture, little by little.

Spoon or pipe the mousse into eight wine glasses and chill for at least 2 hours.

Baked raisin cheesecake

SERVES 8

80g soft cheese

500g fromage blanc

50g crème fraîche

2 large eggs

3 egg yolks

200g caster sugar

½ teaspoon orange zest

½ teaspoon lemon zest

1 teaspoon vanilla extract

35g flour

150g raisins

kirsch

FOR THE PASTRY

60g caster sugar

1 teaspoon grated lemon peel

125g butter, softened, plus extra for greasing

1 egg yolk

10g vanilla sugar

100g flour, plus extra for dusting

Preheat the oven to 190°C/375°F/gas mark 5. Grease a 25cm springform tin with butter.

To make the pastry, put the sugar, lemon peel, softened butter, egg yolk and vanilla sugar in a bowl and blend together. Add the flour and stir well until the mixture is smooth. Roll into a ball, then roll out on a lightly floured surface. Use the pastry to line the bottom of the greased cake tin.

Cream the cheese by whisking it with a fork. Mix in the fromage blanc and crème fraîche. Whisk the eggs and egg yolks together with the sugar, orange and lemon zest, vanilla extract, flour and raisins. Add this mixture to the cheese and cream mixture. Flavour with kirsch.

Fill the pastry with the filling and bake for 1½ hours. After half an hour and during the last hour, remove the cake from the oven at least twice, leaving it to cool for 10 minutes each time.

Brandy snaps

These are by far my favourite childhood treat. I used to be taken to the Maids of Honour tea rooms in Kew and presented with a three-tiered selection of cream cakes and buns. There were always four brandy snaps, with either end dipped in chocolate and filled with stiffly whipped cream. These were the first to go and I'm sure if I'd had the recipe back then, I'd have made them regularly at home.

SERVES 4

50g butter

50g caster sugar

2 level tablespoons golden syrup

50g plain flour

½ tablespoon ground ginger

½ teaspoon brandy

vegetable oil, for brushing

75g dark chocolate

500ml double cream

1 tablespoon icing sugar

Preheat the oven to 180°C/350°F/gas mark 4.

Melt the butter, sugar and syrup until the mixture turns brown. Remove from the heat and stir in the flour and ginger. At this point, the flour will slightly colour the mixture and darken it (don't panic, this is how it should be).

Place tablespoons of the mixture on a baking tray lined with greaseproof paper, allowing it to spread to form small discs. Bake in the oven for 7 to 10 minutes.

Remove from the oven and allow to cool slightly, for about 3 to 4 minutes. Lightly brush the cylindrical handle of a serving spoon or a knife steel with vegetable oil. Roll the discs around the handle to form cylinders. Set aside and allow to cool.

Melt the chocolate in a double boiler. Do not allow the water to boil vigorously or the chocolate will split. Once the chocolate has melted, dip each end of the brandy snaps into the chocolate. Allow the chocolate to set and place to one side.

To fill the brandy snaps, whisk the double cream with the icing sugar until stiff. Put the cream into a piping bag and fill the brandy snaps. You may find it easier to fill half way from each end. Put on to a plate and serve.

ED'S TIP: Always ensure the brandy snaps are cool before you pipe in the cream, but do not refrigerate as the moisture will make them collapse.

Baked orange cheesecake

A heavenly cake, with a devilish white chocolate sauce.

SERVES 8

4 eggs

250g caster sugar

85g flour, sifted, plus extra for
 dusting

pinch of salt

300g cottage cheese

100g ground almonds

125g melted butter plus extra for
 greasing

zest and segments of 4 oranges
 (blood oranges, if possible)

icing sugar, for dusting

FOR THE WHITE CHOCOLATE SAUCE

85g butter

200g white chocolate

100ml single cream, plus extra for
 serving

Preheat the oven to 160°C/325°F/gas mark 3.

Whisk the eggs with a mixer, slowly adding the caster sugar until the mix has quadrupled in volume. Fold in the flour, cottage cheese and almonds. Add the melted butter and orange zest.

Dry the orange segments with kitchen paper, dust them with a little flour and fold through the mixture.

Grease and line a 25cm springform tin and pour in the mixture. Bake for 40 minutes.

For the sauce, melt the butter and chocolate in a heatproof bowl over a pan of simmering water. Once smooth, fold in the single cream.

Remove the cake from the oven, dust with a little icing sugar and serve with the white chocolate sauce and extra cream.

Sourdough starter

Developing a starter is the core to any baker's kitchen. It is relatively straightforward to do and once you have your beloved starter going, you can bake bread on a daily basis using this, rather than yeast. It is an essential ingredient for making sourdough bread, and gives all breads a more natural flavour. It is a far more traditional method for making bread.

You need to approach this as if you're looking after a pet, and quite a difficult pet at that. If neglected, your starter will either die or go completely feral. Once you've developed it, you can keep control by chilling it to slow down its growth.

The basis of a starter is capturing good bacteria in the air and allowing them to feed and grow off the flour and water mixture. If you have healthy bacteria growing, they will happily attack and eat any bad bacteria in the air and will generally come out triumphant in the battle between the two types of bacteria. (The thought of eating bacteria sounds scary, but this is the method used for curing pork, making cheese and of course, bread.)

Growing your own starter may seem like a palaver, but once you get into it, it can become an obsession to keep it going. It sounds odd, but you can become quite fond of this goo growing on top of your mantelpiece and worry about it going hungry or turning bad. Once you get it going, it's quite easy to keep it happy by feeding it once or twice a day.

Wholewheat flour
Still mineral water (always use
 mineral water, as chlorinated or
 treated water will immediately kill
 your starter)

Sterilise a 2-litre pudding basin (see page 235) and put 1 teaspoon of flour and 1 teaspoon of water into it. Stir, using a clean spoon. Place it up on a shelf at room temperature, away from any drafts. Cover with a cheesecloth and leave. After 24 hours, add another teaspoon of flour and a teaspoon of water. Leave and repeat this process on a daily basis.

The starter needs to be fed at least once every 24 hours, with flour and water in equal quantities to your original starter. Therefore it's always best to start with a very small quantity, or before you know it, you'll end up with a bucketfull. By day three, four or five (in summer usually three, in winter five), the bubbles will start to form. Take half of your starter and make your first dough batch. Once you have made the dough, remember to remove a teaspoon to add back to the starter so that you create a genetic line for the remaining use of this starter.

After a week, you will definitely have a pretty successful starter. If you're concerned that it might starve while you're away, or that you might get fed up feeding it or constantly making bread, place it in the fridge to slow down the growth. You will then only have to feed it once a week. If no bubbles appear after three to five days, something's gone wrong and you need to start again.

How do you know if the starter has lost the battle?
Anything other than a cream-coloured or slightly yellow-coloured starter isn't good. It should resemble the consistency of pancake batter. If it separates, don't worry – just gently stir it back together. If mould and fur form on the surface, and it has anything other than sweet-sour smell, it's gone wrong.

If you forget to feed your starter, it is unable to take on the fight with the bad bacteria.

It's best to store it in a glass vessel or pudding basin and keep it covered with a cheesecloth. Although it needs to be fed every 24 hours at the very least, the best time to feed a starter is when it has foamed up, risen and doubled in size. This means that it is growing well and looking for food. If it starts to decrease, this means it's becoming ill and will have completely lost its appetite. Unlike most creatures, it has no immune system and will die very quickly. And yes, you should feel guilty that you've let your beloved starter die, but you just need to start again and wait for another five days.

Sourdough bread

You'll find that this style of loaf appears an awful lot in the book as it's by far my favourite dough recipe.

MAKES 2 LOAVES

7g active dried yeast

235ml lukewarm mineral water

375g sourdough starter (see page 208)

235ml skimmed milk, at room temperature

1 tablespoon honey

1 teaspoon salt

875g flour, plus extra for dusting

In a mixer, combine the yeast with the water. Add the starter and the milk, then the honey and the salt. Add the flour, 1 tablespoon at a time, and beat well with a dough hook to form a smooth dough. You'll need to do this for at least 5 minutes to break the gluten out of the flour. When finished, it should be a smooth and sticky paste, but with a sheen.

Dust a wooden board with flour. Turn the dough out on to the board. Cover loosely with clingfilm and allow to prove for 2 hours.

Preheat the oven to 180°C/350°F/gas mark 4. Punch down the dough and divide it into two balls. Place both on a greased and floured baking tray. Dust the top with either flour or semolina. Let it rise for 30 minutes. Bake for 45 to 60 minutes.

For a soft crust, cool the bread under a dishcloth. For a hard crust, cool without covering.

ED'S TIP: I like to use lard for grease, but you can also use olive oil or margarine.

Beer bread

Goes very well with a ploughman's style lunch. The type of beer used is up to you, you can go as far as to use stout, but I like to use Young's Special.

MAKES 1 LOAF

300g self-raising flour

60g plain flour, plus extra for dusting

55g brown sugar

5g baking powder

pinch of salt

2 tablespoons onion powder

350ml good regional, English ale

50g butter

Preheat the oven to 190°C/375°F/gas mark 5.

Sift the flours into a large bowl. Add the brown sugar, baking powder, salt and onion powder. Make a well in the centre of the dry ingredients. Slowly add the beer while mixing to form a dough. Stir the ingredients until they come together or, alternatively, use a mixer with a dough hook.

On a lightly floured surface, knead the dough for 5 minutes. Shape into an oblong loaf. Lightly grease the inside of a 24 x 12cm loaf tin with butter, and dust with flour. Pop the dough into the loaf tin, making a slit along the top with a sharp knife. Melt the remaining butter and brush it over the surface of the dough.

Bake for 45 to 50 minutes.

Walnut and Stilton bread

A lovely luncheon bread, which goes well with a fresh salad and some pickled onions – no need for cheese!

MAKES 1 LOAF

400g strong white flour, plus extra
  for kneading and rolling

100g strong wholemeal flour

2 sachets dried yeast

½ teaspoon salt

250ml water

75g walnuts

100g Stilton cheese, flaked

Preheat the oven to 200°C/400°F/gas mark 6.

Mix the flours, yeast, salt and water in a large bowl until a soft dough is formed. Place the dough on a lightly floured surface and knead for 5 minutes. Alternatively, use a mixer with a dough hook.

Put the dough on a floured surface and, using a rolling pin, roll out into a large sheet, 4cm thick. Sprinkle with walnuts and flakes of Stilton.

Roll the dough back up into a cylinder shape. Fold it in half over itself and place in a bowl. Cover with clingfilm and allow to rise for 1 hour.

Remove the dough from the bowl, and re-shape to form a ball. Score the top with a cross, place on to a floured baking tray and bake for 30 minutes until brown.

Cool on a wire rack.

Corn bread and baked beans

Beans and corn bread had a fight, cos beans and
corn bread were out on a Friday night.

MAKES 1 LOAF

100g butter, melted, plus 25g
 unmelted for greasing

375g plain flour

225g cornmeal

1 tablespoon salt

4 tablespoons baking powder

100g sugar

400ml milk

200ml buttermilk (see tip)

2 eggs

50g margarine

Preheat the oven to 200°C/400°F/gas mark 6.
Grease a 23cm square loaf tin. In a large bowl,
combine all the ingredients together. Mix until you
have the consistency of a sponge cake batter, then
pour into the prepared loaf tin.

Bake for about 20 minutes in the top of the
oven. The corn bread is ready when it is golden
and springy to the touch. Cover with a cloth
immediately to prevent the bread from becoming
hard while cooling.

ED'S TIP: If you don't have buttermilk, just increase
the milk to 475ml.

Potato bread

Although making this bread is quite a long and drawn out process, and a relatively complicated one too, it is, in my opinion, the finest bread one can make. I think anyone who eats it will agree.

MAKES 1 LARGE LOAF

1 medium potato, sliced

¼ tablespoon instant yeast

good pinch of caster sugar

700g unbleached flour, plus extra for
   rolling and dusting

pinch of salt

2 tablespoons honey

Boil the potato in 550ml of water, then drain and reserve this water (approx. 500ml).

Add the yeast to the potato water, along with the sugar and then add one third of this yeasted water to 100g flour. Beat well until combined, cover and leave to ferment for 2 hours. Then add the potato. This mixture is 'the foundation'.

Make the dough using a mixer with a dough hook. Mix the remaining flour, the salt, 200ml of the remaining potato water and the honey together. Keep the dough in the bowl, cover and let rest for 30 minutes.

Mix in the foundation with the dough hook. Work it for at least 5 minutes until it becomes a silky smooth dough.

Remove the dough from the machine, set it on a well-floured board and let it rest for 10 minutes. Shape into a large, round ball and dust with flour. Put into a container three times its size and cover with clingfilm. Turn the dough at 20 minutes intervals four times, then leave for 3½ hours.

Turn out the dough on to a floured surface. Using your hands, make a hole in the centre all the way through to make a ring. Cover loosely with clingfilm and allow to rise for 1 hour.

Preheat the oven to 230°C/450°F/gas mark 8 or as high it will go. Ideally, place a baking stone on the central shelf (if you do not have one, use a baking tray) and heat it in the oven while you flour a large piece of greaseproof paper. Flip the bread on to this, turning it as you do so that the bottom becomes the top.

To bake, lightly dust the top of the bread with flour and slash four times around the ring. Remove the hot stone or tray from the oven and slide the bread onto it. Cook for 40 to 50 minutes until dark brown, then cool on a wire rack.

Soda bread

MAKES 1 LOAF

325g granary flour

50g self-raising flour

1 teaspoon bicarbonate of soda

1 teaspoon salt

150ml yoghurt

50ml milk

Preheat the oven to 180˚C/350˚F/gas mark 4.

In a bowl, mix the granary flour with the self-raising flour, bicarbonate of soda and salt. Add the yoghurt and the milk and mix together, forming into a dough. Knead for 1 minute, then let it sit for 10 minutes.

Form the dough into a round shape and place on to a baking tray. Sprinkle with flour and bake for 20 to 25 minutes.

Tomato bread

MAKES 1 LOAF

15g fresh yeast

100ml extra virgin olive oil

500g white bread flour, plus extra for kneading

1 teaspoon salt

2 tomatoes, thinly sliced

pinch of salt

good pinch of dried oregano

In a large mixing bowl, mix the yeast with 140ml cold water to form a paste. Add another 140ml cold water, with 1 tablespoon of the olive oil and mix together. Add half the flour and the salt. Blend well. Start to work in the rest of the flour to form a soft dough. Tip the dough out on to a lightly floured work surface and knead. Alternatively, this can be done in a food mixer with a dough hook from the very beginning.

Grease an oven tray and dust it lightly with flour. Put the dough on it and cover with a damp tea towel. Allow to rise for 1 hour. Remove the tea towel and, using your fingers, make firm indentations all over the dough. Again, cover with a tea towel and allow to rise for another hour.

Preheat the oven to 220˚C/425˚F/gas mark 7. Drizzle the surface of the bread with 1 tablespoon olive oil. Sprinkle with sea salt. Flick the surface of the bread with cold water and bake for 5 minutes.

Remove from the oven, cover the surface of the bread with thinly sliced tomatoes, a good pinch of salt and oregano. Drizzle with the remainder of the olive oil and bake for a further 25 minutes until golden brown.

Bung-it-in bread

With rising food prices, we're all shocked sometimes at what we have to spend on our weekly food shop. Our throw-it-away mentality needs to change to run a household on a budget. A great way of doing this is to use up leftovers, such as green beans, olives and potatoes baked into a loaf. The bread makes a great on-the-move snack or lunch – the only other ingredient needed is butter. Just about anything can go into a loaf, but I suggest it is always cut up into smallish pieces first. Adding your leftover ingredients first to the flour stops them sinking whilst the dough rises.

MAKES 1 LOAF

1 tablespoon margarine or beef
   dripping, plus extra for greasing
275g leftover fresh vegetables, such
   as a mix of green beans, olives, red
   pepper and/or potato, cut into small
   pieces
400g strong white flour, plus extra
   for dusting
175g wholemeal flour
10g salt
25g fresh yeast or 7g packet dried
   yeast

Line a large baking sheet with greaseproof paper. Grease the paper with margarine or beef dripping and dust with flour.

Place all the leftover food into a large sieve and hold over a bowl. Sprinkle over the flours and sift gently, allowing some flour to stick to the leftovers as it falls through into the bowl. Add the salt, yeast and 250ml water to the bowl. Place the sieve to one side.

Knead for 5 minutes to form a dough. If the dough seems a little loose, add another 2 tablespoons flour during the kneading process.

During the last minute of kneading, add the margarine or beef dripping. Remove the dough to a floured surface and roll out to 2cm thick. Scatter over the leftover food and gently bring the corners in. Fold the bread in on itself again and place the loaf upside down on to the prepared baking sheet. Dust with flour, cover with clingfilm, and allow to rise for 1½ hours.

Preheat the oven to 190°C/375°F/gas mark 5. Once risen, bake the loaf for 50 minutes. Remove to a cooling rack and cover with a tea towel. Slice and serve with butter.

Fruit bread

MAKES 2 LOAVES

900g plain flour, plus extra for
   dusting
1 teaspoon salt
50g butter, plus extra for greasing
425ml lukewarm milk
1 teaspoon yeast
50g soft brown sugar
1 egg, beaten
30g mixed dried fruit

Preheat oven to 200°C/400°F/gas mark 6.

Mix the flour and salt and rub in the butter. Pour 150ml of the milk over the yeast, add the sugar and leave for a few minutes, then beat it with a fork. Leave in a warm place to froth.

Add the egg and the remaining milk to the flour, then the yeast mixture, a little at a time (note that you may not need to use all the liquid). Knead for 5 minutes, mix in the dried fruit and cover the dough with clingfilm. Put in a warm place for 20 minutes.

Turn out on to a floured board. Knead for a few minutes. Put into two greased 450g loaf tins. Return to a warm place and leave for about an hour to double in size.

Bake for 35 minutes and turn out while warm.

Milk dough buns

MAKES 12 BUNS

1 teaspoon dried yeast
300ml lukewarm milk
25g soft brown sugar
450g plain white flour, plus extra for
   dusting
1 teaspoon salt
50g butter

Preheat the oven to 200°C/400°F/gas mark 6.

Sprinkle the yeast over half the milk and leave for a few minutes. Beat with a fork and add the sugar. Put in a warm place to froth for 15 to 20 minutes.

Mix together the flour and salt and rub in the butter. Pour the frothed milk and yeast on to the flour. Add the remaining milk and beat by hand for a few minutes. Place in bowl and cover with clingfilm. Allow to rise in a warm place for 1 hour.

To make the buns, break the dough into 5cm portions. (You should be able to make 12 buns out of this mixture.) Dust a surface with flour, roll the dough portions into balls and then lay them out on the floured surface.

Grease a baking tray with 1 tablespoon vegetable oil and cover with greaseproof paper. Transfer the balls to the baking tray and lightly dust with flour. Cover loosely with clingfilm and allow to double in size, for approximately 40 minutes.

Bake for 30 minutes and turn out while warm.

Teatime bread

MAKES 1 LOAF

50g butter, plus extra for greasing
700g self-raising flour
pinch of salt
150g soft brown sugar
100g raisins
1 egg, beaten well
225ml milk
200ml golden syrup, warmed

Preheat the oven to 180°C/350°F/gas mark 4.

Rub the butter into the flour. Add the salt, sugar and raisins. Add the egg, milk and warmed golden syrup to the mixture and stir to combine.

Spoon the mixture into two greased, rectangular 15cm loaf tins. Bake at once for 1½ hours.

Turn out while warm, cut into slices and enjoy with butter.

Shortcrust pastry

MAKES ABOUT 350G
225g flour
pinch of salt
110g butter, chopped and softened
1 egg yolk
3 tablespoons iced water

Sift the flour and salt into a bowl. Rub in the butter pieces. Add the egg yolk and iced water.

Gently bring together with your hands to form a rough pastry. There's no need to knead it or work it as this will make it brittle.

Wrap in clingfilm and chill for 30 minutes before using.

ED'S TIP: Any leftover pastry can be kept in the freezer until the next time you bake a tart or pie.

Sweet pastry

MAKES ABOUT 800G
450g flour
140g caster sugar
pinch of salt
225g unsalted butter, cubed and
  chilled
1 egg
1 tablespoon orange zest
1 tablespoon iced water

Sift the flour into a large bowl, then add the sugar and salt. Mix together.

Add the cubes of chilled butter, using your fingertips to rub into the flour until you have a breadcrumb consistency.

In a separate bowl, whisk the egg and orange zest together and add the iced water. Add this to the flour mixture, mixing until you have a light dough.

Wrap in clingfilm and place in the fridge for at least 30 minutes before using.

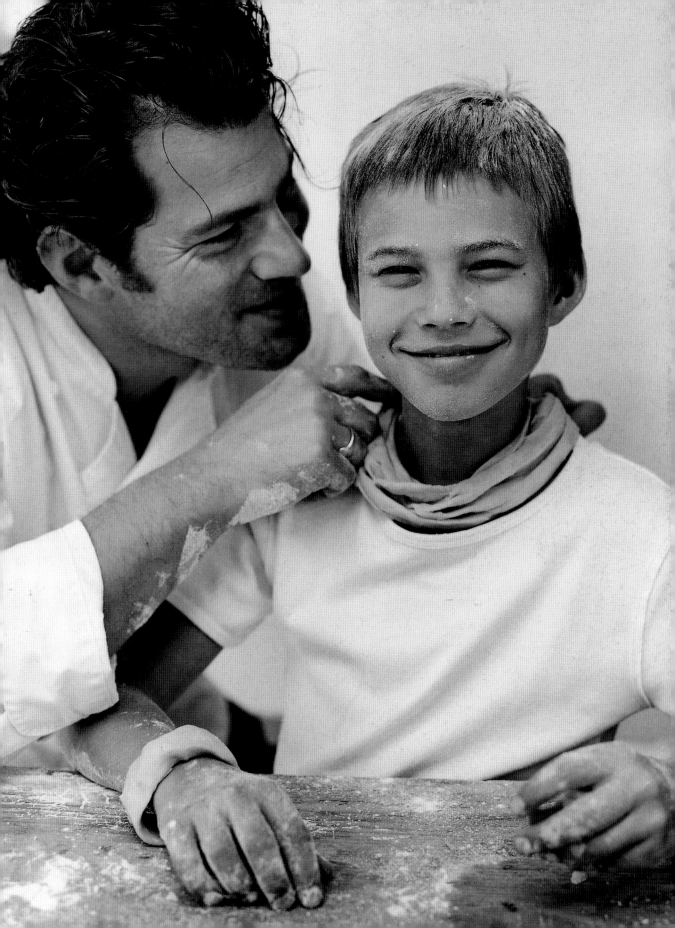

Puff pastry

MAKES ABOUT 550G

225g plain flour, plus extra for
  dusting

good pinch of salt

200g butter, placed in the freezer for
  1 hour

1 tablespoon iced water

juice of ½ lemon

1 egg, beaten

150g cold butter, thinly sliced

Sift the flour and the salt together into a large mixing bowl. Coarsely grate the hardened butter into the flour.

Mix the iced water and the lemon juice and add to the flour mixture along with the egg. Using a palette knife, cut everything together to make a dryish dough, and pat together.

Turn the dough out on to a floured surface and roll it out. Dot the surface with some of the thin slices of butter, then fold the pastry over on to itself. Then repeat, dotting the surface with more slices of butter, and fold the pastry towards you.

Gently roll out the pastry again and repeat this process until all the butter is incorporated.

Wrap in clingfilm and chill for at least 1 hour before using.

English rough puff pastry

MAKES ABOUT 1KG

450g strong plain flour

pinch of salt

225g lard, placed in the freezer for
  1 hour

225g margarine, placed in the freezer
  for 1 hour

275ml iced water

squeeze of lemon juice

Sift the flour and salt into a large bowl, and grate in the lard and margarine. Add the iced water and a squeeze of lemon juice.

Make cuts across the mixture with a palette knife, while turning the bowl to ensure everything is combined. Pat together to form a dough, then place to chill in the fridge.

Turn the dough out on to a floured surface and roll out into a rectangle 3cm thick. Fold the bottom edge over into the middle of the rectangle, and then fold the top edge in so that the edges touch. Press the edges together with a rolling pin, then chill.

Dust the rolling pin lightly with flour and roll the dough out into a rectangle 3cm thick. Fold the top edge in as before, and then the bottom edge, sealing the dough where they meet. Then chill.

Repeat these steps three more times, chilling each time in between. Chill the dough overnight.

Hot water pastry

This is what encases our famous pork pies.

MAKES ABOUT 550G

150g lard

400g plain flour

½ tablespoon salt

Warm the lard with 125ml water in a saucepan over a gentle heat – do not boil. Ensure the lard melts.

Sift the flour into a bowl and add the salt. Pour over the hot water and lard and mix together until you've formed a dough. If it has a greasy consistency, add another tablespoon of flour and knead again.

Leave for a while until the dough has cooled to body temperature – don't let it cool down any more than that. Roll the pastry out and use as required.

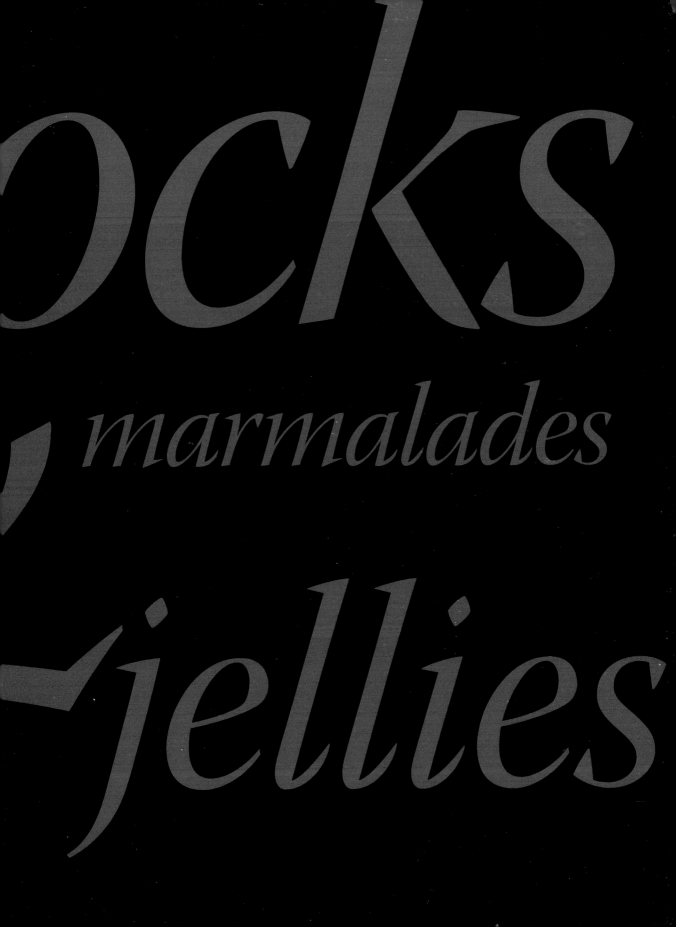

Beef stock

MAKES 1 LITRE
1kg beef bones
1 carrot, roughly chopped
2 celery sticks, roughly chopped
1 onion, roughly chopped
¾ bottle red wine
bouquet garni (see tip)
salt and freshly ground black pepper

Preheat the oven to 200°C/400°F/gas mark 6.

Place the beef bones and vegetables in a roasting tray and roast for about 30 minutes until caramelised.

Pour half the bottle of red wine into a pan. Bring to the boil, add the roasted beef bones, vegetables and the bouquet garni. Top up with the remaining wine and enough water to cover the bones.

Simmer for 4 hours, periodically skimming any scum off the surface. Strain the stock into a clean saucepan, reduce by half.

ED'S TIP: Tie a sprig of fresh parsley, thyme, rosemary and a bay leaf together to make a fresh and aromatic bouquet garni.

Chicken stock

MAKES 3 LITRES
2kg chicken wings
vegetable oil
2 carrots, tops on
1 leek
1 onion
2 celery sticks
4 garlic cloves
bunch of fresh thyme
1 bay leaf
1 tablespoon black peppercorns

Preheat the oven to 220°C/425°F/gas mark 7. Place the chicken wings in an oiled roasting tin and roast for about 45 minutes or until brown.

Remove the chicken wings from the oven and place in a large pan. Add 4 litres of water and bring to the boil. Skim off any scum from the surface, then reduce to a simmer. Add all the remaining ingredients and bring back to the boil. Skim off any remaining scum and reduce to a gentle simmer for 3 to 4 hours. Strain through a sieve before using it.

Fish stock

MAKES 850ML
3 tablespoons Pernod or dry sherry
1kg bones from non-oily fish (see tip)
2 carrots, roughly chopped
1 onion, quartered
2 celery sticks, roughly chopped
tops of 2 fennel bulbs or 4 star anise
8 black peppercorns
1 bay leaf
small bunch of fresh parsley
1 garlic clove

Pour the sherry or Pernod into a saucepan. Bring to the boil and then remove from the heat. Add all the remaining ingredients to the saucepan. Pour over 850ml water and bring to the boil.

As soon as the liquid has reached the boil, turn down to a low simmer, skim off the scum that has formed on the surface and cook for 20 minutes.

Strain through a sieve into a bowl and allow to cool. Once cooled, ladle into a container, leaving any sediment in the base of the bowl, and refrigerate or freeze.

ED'S TIP: The fish stall at your local market or supermarket will usually give you fish bones for free – just ask.

Lamb stock

MAKES 1 LITRE
1kg lamb bones
1 carrot, roughly chopped
2 celery sticks, roughly chopped
1 onion, roughly chopped
¾ bottle red wine
bouquet garni
200ml port
1 teaspoon redcurrant jelly
salt and freshly ground black pepper

Preheat the oven to 200°C/400°F/gas mark 6.

Place the lamb bones and vegetables in a roasting tray and roast for about 30 minutes until caramelised.

Pour half the bottle of red wine into a pan. Bring to the boil, add the roasted beef bones, vegetables and the bouquet garni. Top up with the remaining wine and enough water to cover the bones.

Simmer the stock for 4 hours, periodically skimming any scum off the surface. Strain the stock into a pan and stir in the port and redcurrant jelly. Reduce by half and season to taste and refrigerate or freeze.

Vegetable stock

MAKES 1 LITRE
1 leek, thoroughly rinsed and roughly chopped
5 celery sticks, roughly chopped
3 carrots, roughly chopped
1 onion, roughly chopped

Place all the ingredients into a large saucepan with 1.2 litres of water. Bring to the boil, then turn the heat down and simmer gently for 2 hours.

Strain through a sieve into a bowl and allow to cool. Once cooled, ladle into a container and refrigerate or freeze.

ED'S TIP: If you reduce the stock all the way down to about 200ml, you can pour it into a ice cube tray and freeze, for your homemade version of a stock cube. When you want to use the stock, just bring a cube to the boil with 200ml water.

Onion gravy

Although traditionally served with the finest quality sausages, this gravy goes well with pretty much any meat: try it with calves' liver, pan-fried kidneys or grilled beef steak.

MAKES 200ML
vegetable oil
2 onions, peeled and sliced
1 tablespoon plain flour
1 tablespoon tomato purée
2 garlic cloves, lightly crushed
sprig of oregano
½ bottle red wine
375ml good beef stock (see page 230) or veal stock
salt and freshly ground black pepper

Heat 2 tablespoons of vegetable oil in a frying pan and fry the onions until almost brown and crisp. These are known as 'tobacco onions'.

Add the flour, tomato purée and garlic. Cook gently for 3 to 4 minutes, stirring occasionally. Add the oregano and gradually pour in the wine, stirring constantly to prevent any lumps from forming. Bring to the boil and reduce by half.

Add the stock, bring back to a simmer and reduce by three quarters, skimming off any scum that rises to the surface.

Remove the garlic and the oregano and season to taste.

ED'S TIP: You can buy delicious veal stock in the supermarkets, if you don't feel like making the stock yourself.

Red gooseberry jelly

MAKES 4 X 400ML JARS
500g red gooseberries, washed,
   topped and tailed
500ml clear apple juice
1 vanilla pod, seeds scraped out
about 300g caster sugar

Put the gooseberries into a heavy-based saucepan
and pour over the apple juice. Put both the vanilla
pod and the seeds into the saucepan, and boil for 15
minutes. Strain the pulp through a jelly bag (or use
a colander, lined with several layers of muslin cloth)
for 2 hours without stirring or pushing it through.

Measure the extract. For every 100ml extract,
add 70g sugar. Now simmer the extract with the
sugar for about 15 minutes until the setting point is
reached (see tip). While simmering, de-scum the
mixture regularly with a large spoon.

Pour into sterilised jars (see tip page 235).

ED'S TIP: To check the setting point, put a small
dollop of jelly on to a plate and into the fridge for
2 minutes. Touch the jelly with the back of a spoon
and pull up. If it lifts up like a thread, it has reached
setting point.

Apple compote

MAKES 200ML
2 Bramley cooking apples
100ml sweet cider
1 tablespoon white sugar
1 teaspoon cider vinegar
pinch of salt

Peel and core the apples, then cut into cubes. Place
into a saucepan and add the cider, sugar, vinegar
and salt. Bring to the boil, then cook gently for
20 minutes. Leave to cool, then scoop into a jar and
store in the fridge. It'll keep for three days or so.

Damson and rosemary jelly

MAKES ABOUT 600ML
900g damsons
4 sprigs of fresh rosemary
juice of ½ lemon
450g white sugar

Place all ingredients except the sugar in a saucepan
with just enough water to cover. Bring to the boil and
simmer for an hour, stirring from time to time.

Allow to cool. Over a bowl, ladle the liquid into
either a jelly bag or a colander lined with several
layers of muslin cloth. Stir the damson pulp gently
and then leave to strain overnight.

Discard the pulp and measure out 600ml damson
liquid – if you have slightly less, top up with water.

Pour into a saucepan and add the sugar. Stir over
a gentle heat until the sugar has dissolved. Bring to
a vigorous boil, stirring constantly to ensure it does
not burn. Be careful as it will get quite hot.

The damson jelly is ready when a spoon, drawn
across the base of the pan, makes a clear track mark.
Put the jelly in sterilised jars (see tip page 235).

Onion marmalade

MAKES 2 X 400ML JARS
175g demerara sugar
450g English onions, sliced
50ml red wine vinegar
1 bay leaf
50ml Pedro Ximénez sherry

Place the sugar in a saucepan and cook over a medium to low heat until it caramelises.

Add the onions and cook until softened in the sugar. Add the vinegar and bay leaf and gently simmer for 15 minutes.

Stir in the sherry and bring back to the boil, then remove from the heat. Allow to cool and serve.

Cumberland sauce

MAKES 200ML
4 small oranges
2 lemons
1 shallot, finely chopped
50g unsalted butter
2 tablespoons port
5cm piece of fresh ginger, chopped
1 teaspoon English mustard powder
2 pinches of cayenne pepper
4 tablespoons redcurrant jelly

Carefully peel the outer skins from the orange and the lemon and cut into fine shreds. Squeeze the oranges and lemons and discard the pips.

Sweat the shallots in the butter until softened. Add the peel and juice, and then the port, ginger, mustard and cayenne. Cook gently for 5 minutes.

Add the redcurrant jelly and stir thoroughly to ensure the jelly has dissolved into the sauce. Remove from the heat and allow to cool completely.

Stored in a jar, it'll keep in the fridge three days.

Quick marmalade

MAKES 8 X 400ML JARS

1.3kg Seville oranges

2.25kg granulated sugar

very finely grated zest and juice of 2
  lemons

1 miniature bottle of orange liqueur

Put the oranges and 1.2 litres of water in a large
saucepan. Bring to the boil, cover with a tight-fitting
lid and simmer for 1 hour until very soft. Lift out the
oranges, reserving the cooking liquid.

Once cool enough to handle, cut the oranges
in half. Remove the pips and scoop out the flesh,
adding it back into the saucepan with the cooking
liquid. Add 600ml water and cook for 10 minutes,
then strain and reserve the liquid.

Scrape the softened orange peel to remove the
pith, then chop the peel with a knife for a coarse cut
or push it through a mincer for a fine cut. Return
the peel to the pan with the strained liquid.

Add the sugar and lemon zest. Pour the lemon
juice through a strainer into the pan. Stir together
over a low heat until the sugar has dissolved, then
bring to the boil. Cook rapidly until the liquid has
set (see tip page 232) – this takes about 20 minutes.

Take the pan off the heat. Spoon off the
scum that has risen to the surface and allow the
marmalade to stand for 20 minutes to cool. (This
ensures even distribution of the peel.)

Stir in the liqueur, and ladle into warm sterilised
jars (see tip page 235). Cover with wax circles while
still hot and then wait to seal until cold.

Crab apple and lavender jelly

MAKES 6 X 500ML JARS

4kg crab apples, any bruises or pits
  cut out

20 lavender flower heads

about 1kg caster sugar

juice of 1 lemon

Put the apples in a saucepan with the lavender.
Cover with water, bring to the boil and simmer
for 30 minutes. Pour the pulp into a jelly bag (or
use a colander, lined with several layers of muslin
cloth) over a bucket. Allow to drip overnight (don't
squeeze the apples as this will cloud the jelly).

The following day, measure the amount of juice.
For every 10 parts of juice, add 7 parts of sugar and
combine them in a large saucepan.

Add the lemon juice and bring to the boil,
stirring to dissolve the sugar. Keep at a rolling

boil for 35 to 40 minutes, skimming off the froth regularly.

Remove from the heat, allow to cool and pour the warm liquid into sterilised preserving jars (see tip). Tightly seal the lids whilst still warm. Label and then store the jars in a cool, dry place.

ED'S TIP: The old-fashioned way to sterilise jars is to boil them, with their lids, in boiling water for 5 minutes. An easier way is to run them through the dishwasher on a hot cycle. Allow the jars to cool for 10 minutes and then cover the filling with disks of greaseproof paper and screw on the lids.

Mint sauce

Nothing beats a homemade mint sauce. Grow and chop your own mint or buy a nice big bunch – it's one of nature's greatest herbs.

SERVES 4
75ml red wine vinegar
25g sugar
1 small red onion, finely chopped
50g fresh mint, finely chopped
good pinch of salt

Combine the vinegar, sugar and onion together in a saucepan. Bring to the boil and allow to simmer gently for 5 minutes. Remove from the heat. Add the mint and salt.

Cool, pour into a jar and chill in the fridge. Mint sauce loses its flavour when kept for too long, so it's always best to make it fresh.

index